THE ORIGIN OF THE PROLOGUE
TO ST JOHN'S GOSPEL

THE ORIGIN OF THE PROLOGUE
TO ST JOHN'S GOSPEL

by

RENDEL HARRIS

WIPF & STOCK · Eugene, Oregon

Wipf and Stock Publishers
199 W 8th Ave, Suite 3
Eugene, OR 97401

The Origin of the Prologue to St. John's Gospel
By Harris, J. Rendel
Softcover ISBN-13: 978-1-6667-3561-1
Hardcover ISBN-13: 978-1-6667-9286-7
eBook ISBN-13: 978-1-6667-9287-4
Publication date 10/12/2021
Previously published by Cambridge University Press, 1917

This edition is a scanned facsimile of
the original edition published in 1917.

PREFACE

IN the following pages I have gathered together and made some additions to a series of articles which I recently published in the pages of the *Expositor*. If I am right in the results here reached, we must recognise that a fresh chapter has been added to the *History of Christian Dogma*, and one that stands very near to the beginning of the book. A nearer approach to the origin of the Christology of the Church means a closer approximation to the position of those who first tried to answer the question "Who do men say that I am?"; and to be nearer the Apostles is to be nearer, also, to Christ Himself. It is not easy to say how much of the argument is really new; as far as I know, British theologians have hardly touched the question, they are always more at home in the fourth century than in the first! The best account of the subject that I have come across is Lebreton's *Origines du dogme de la Trinité*, which combines Catholic doctrine with a good deal of sound reasoning as to the evolution of that doctrine I should have quoted it several times if I had read it before my brief essay was written. As it is, I can only refer to it here, without suggesting that my commendations should be reckoned along with the imprimatur under which it appears. They are appreciations rather than endorsements. It is certainly a book from which very much can be learned by students of every school of thought. While these pages are passing through the press I have had the pleasure of examining Prof. Hans Windisch's essay on *Die göttliche Weisheit der Juden und die paulinische Christologie*, in which a number of the conclusions in this book are either adumbrated, or definitely stated. It would have been easy for Prof. Windisch to carry his argument further, if he had known the bearing of the early *Testimony Book* upon the Christological problem.

In theology generally we seem to be at a standstill from which we can only be moved by the discovery of fresh facts, or the opening up of fresh lines of enquiry. It will certainly be to many a discovery that Jesus was known in the first century as the Wisdom of God; with equal certainty the application of this new fact to the existing Christian tradition will be productive of not a little motion amongst its dry bones.

My thanks are due to the Editor of the *Expositor*, from whose pages much of the following volume is reproduced, and to my friend Vacher Burch, who has assisted me greatly in the composition and correction of the volume.

RENDEL HARRIS.

October, 1916.

CONTENTS

	PAGE
THE ORIGIN OF THE PROLOGUE TO ST JOHN, I . .	1
,, ,, , II .	19
,, ,, ,, III	24
CHRIST AS THE HAND OF GOD	43
ON THE ASCRIPTION OF SAPIENTIAL TITLES TO CHRIST	52
DID JESUS CALL HIMSELF SOPHIA? . .	57
ST JOHN AND THE DIVINE WISDOM .	62

THE ORIGIN OF THE PROLOGUE TO ST JOHN'S GOSPEL

I

In a recent number of the *Commonwealth*, Professor Scott Holland writes with enthusiasm in praise of the Poet Laureate's new book *The Spirit of Man*. But he says that he has one real regret and one only He regrets that Dr Bridges was persuaded to give the opening passage of St John's Gospel as "In the beginning was mind." The criticism here made, which I quote from that excellent little paper, entitled *Public Opinion* (as I have no access to the *Commonwealth*), raises once more in our minds the question as to the real meaning and the actual genesis of the Prologue to the Fourth Gospel. Are we nearer to the actual sense of the words when we say with the Poet Laureate that "in the beginning was Mind," or, as some would say, "in the beginning was Thought," or are we to say with Professor Scott Holland that *Mind* is an inadequate term, and that the idea must have included "speech, expression, the rational word"?

It seems evident that there must be other questions to be resolved before we come to the hermeneutical and exegetical problems over which the Professor and the Poet are in danger of a collision For instance, we want to know more about this Prologue, which is attributed commonly to St John, and which, in any case, contains theological statements of the highest importance, deserving, if any such statements necessarily deserve, an apostolical authority Is this Prologue an intellectual Athena bursting forth suddenly from the brain of a mystical Zeus? or is it, like so many other surprising statements of poets, sages and saints which seem to defy evolution and to be as independent of ancestry as Melchizedek, a statement which carries about it, upon close examination, marks of an ancestry in stages and by steps, like most of the religious, intellectual and physical products with which we are acquainted?

To put it another way. The Church is firmly persuaded, and not without strong supporting reasons, that these opening sentences of the Fourth Gospel are among the most inspired words in the whole of the Christian records. It is not merely that they have resonance, and apparent novelty, and depth of meaning, and unexpected views of the world *sub specie aeternitatis* They are so unlike any other evangelical prologues: their *Beginning* is not the "Genesis of Jesus Christ" in Matthew, nor the *Beginning of the Gospel* in Mark; their glory of the Son of God is not the abrupt formula with which Mark opens, and which he uses his pictorial records to attest: the artistic fashion of them does not appear to be made on the lines of some previously successful literary artist, like the elegant Greek of the first verses of St Luke Is it any wonder that direct and immediate inspiration has been claimed for these majestic sentences? Thus Jerome, in his prologue to Matthew, speaks of St John as *saturatus revelatione* when he wrote his opening words: and it is possible that the same sense of constraint is involved in the terms in which Jerome describes St John as setting pen to paper,

in illud proemium caelo veniens
eructavit In principio erat verbum:

but this ought not to be unduly pressed, since Jerome's *eructavit* is really borrowed from the opening of Psalm xlv :

Eructavit cor meum *verbum* bonum,

where the language is taken to express the emission of the doctrine of the Logos by St John, and goes back to the Septuagint, ἐξηρεύξατο ἡ καρδία μου λόγον ἀγαθόν However that may be, it is certain that the Prologue of St John is the high-water mark of inspiration for those who read the Scriptures reverently.

It is just at this point that the enquiring mind puts in a protest and asks whether it is not possible that, conceding the inspiration of the words, we might legitimately question the immediateness of the inspiration. Suppose then we go in search of any prior stages of thought that may underlie the famous Prologue To begin with, there is the description of Christ as the Logos Was that reached immediately, as soon as Philosophy and Religion looked one another fairly in the face in Ephesus or Palestine, or Alexandria? How soon did the term "Word of God" acquire a metaphysical sense? The question is, perhaps, easier asked than answered. In the Synoptic Gospels the term "Word of God" is always used of the utterance divine or the record of that utterance It is that which the sower sows, that which the traditionalist makes void by his tradition, that which the multitudes throng round Jesus to hear. And the curious thing is that in the Fourth Gospel there is a similar usage, after one passes away from the Prologue and the doctrine of the Incarnation Jesus Himself speaks of the readers of a certain Psalm as those to whom the Word of God came, and of His own message (rather than Himself) as the Word of the Father which He has communicated to His disciples "I have given them thy word[1]." The suggestion is natural that we should regard the philosophical use of Logos as the latest deposit upon the surface of the narration, a verbal usage which has displaced an earlier meaning and sense. It is the more curious that the Evangelist never reverts to the Logos with which he opens his narrative, in view of the fact that Christ speaks as "Light" and "Life" in various parts of the Gospel, and so identifies Himself (or is identified) with the metaphysic of the Prologue

Is it possible, we ask next, that the Logos may have displaced an earlier metaphysical title as well as that employment of the word which we usually indicate by not writing it in capitals?

All through the rest of the New Testament the Word of God means the Evangelic message, except in one passage in the Apocalypse, where it is a title of the Messiah, and a doubtful place in Hebrews where the "quick and powerful" word of God appears to be explicable by Philonean parallels in a metaphysical sense

We find, however, that there is occasionally another title given to Jesus Christ. He is called "*the Wisdom of God* and the Power of God," and is said to become the *Wisdom of his people*. "He has become to us Wisdom[2]" So the question arises whether Sophia may not be an alternative title to Logos and perhaps prior to it

For instance, in the Gospel of Luke (xi 49) the Wisdom of God is personified and speaks of sending prophets and wise men to be

---

[1] John xvii 14, where the sense of λόγος is fixed by the alternative ῥήματα of verse 8.

[2] 1 Cor i 30, where the use of the conjunctions makes it clear that the emphasis is on Wisdom, which should have a capital letter, and be explained by "righteousness, sanctification and redemption" See Moffatt *in loc.*

rejected by the scribes and Pharisees Apparently this is not meant for a Biblical quotation, and in that sense is not the Word of God; the "Wisdom" that speaks is not the title nor the contents of a book. In the corresponding passage of Matthew (I suppose we must refer the origin to the lost document Q) we have simply "Therefore, behold! I send unto you, etc." So when Tatian made his Harmony, he naturally produced the sentence, "Behold! I, the Wisdom of God, send unto you, etc.," which brings out clearly the involved, personified Wisdom—Christ, and inasmuch as God is personified and speaks through Sophia, when He sends His processional array of prophets and wise men, we have what in Greek looks like a feminine form of the Johannine Logos The suggestion arises (at present in the form of a pure hypothesis) that *the way to Logos is through Sophia and that the latter is the ancestress of the former* Now let us try if we can re-write the Johannine Prologue, substituting the word Sophia for the word Logos. It now runs as follows—

> In the beginning was the Divine Wisdom,
> and Wisdom was with God,
> and Wisdom was God.
> The same was in the beginning with God·
> All things were made by her, and without her was nothing made that was made

As soon as we have written down the sentences we are at once struck by their resemblance to the Old Testament: we could almost say that we were transcribing a famous passage in Proverbs:

> Prov viii 22-30 "The Lord possessed me (Sophia) *in the beginning* of his way, before his works of old. I was set up from everlasting, *from the beginning* ...when he prepared the heavens *I was there* when he set a compass upon the face of the deep.. then *I was by him*."

It seems clear that we have found the stratum of the Old Testament upon which the Prologue reposes. This is practically admitted by almost all persons who find Old Testament references in the New: they simply cannot ignore the eighth chapter of Proverbs If this be so, and if the Logos is quoted as being and doing just what Sophia is said to be and to do in the Book of Proverbs, then the equation between Logos and Sophia is justified, and we may speak of Christ in the metaphysical sense as the Wisdom of God, and may write out the first draft of the doctrine of the Logos in the form which we have suggested above. In other words, we have

THE ORIGIN OF THE PROLOGUE TO ST JOHN

in the Prologue not an immediate oracle, but a mediated one, in which separate stages can be marked out, and an original groundform postulated. Now let us examine the Greek of the Prologue and compare it with the Greek of the Septuagint in Proverbs. We readily see the principal parallels consist in the collocation of—

$$\begin{cases} \underline{\dot{\epsilon}ν\ \dot{α}ρχῇ}\ ἦν\ \dot{o}\ λόγος\ \text{and} \\ κύριος\ \dot{\epsilon}κτισ\dot{\epsilon}ν\ με\ \dot{α}ρχὴν\ \dot{o}δῶν\ αὐτοῦ \qquad πρὸ\ τοῦ\ αἰῶνος\ \dot{\epsilon}θεμελίωσ\dot{\epsilon}ν\ με \\ \underline{\dot{\epsilon}ν\ \dot{α}ρχῇ} \qquad\qquad\qquad\qquad\qquad\qquad\qquad\qquad (\text{viii } 22) \end{cases}$$

$$\begin{cases} \dot{o}\ λόγος\ ἦν\ \underline{πρὸς\ τὸν\ θεόν}\ \text{and} \\ ἤμην\ \underline{παρ'\ αὐτῷ} \qquad\qquad\qquad\qquad\qquad\qquad\qquad (\text{viii. 30}) \end{cases}$$

$$\begin{cases} οὗτος\ ἦν\ \underline{\dot{\epsilon}ν\ \dot{α}ρχῇ}\ \underline{πρὸς\ τὸν\ θεόν}\ \text{and} \\ ἡνίκα\ ἡτοίμαζεν\ τὸν\ οὐρανόν,\ \underline{συμπαρήμην\ αὐτῷ} \qquad (\text{viii. 27}) \\ \text{cf. also}\ \dot{o}\ θεὸς\ τῇ\ σοφίᾳ\ \dot{\epsilon}θεμελίωσεν\ τὴν\ γῆν \qquad (\text{iii 19}) \end{cases}$$

$$\begin{cases} \dot{\epsilon}ν\ αὐτῷ\ \underline{ζωὴ}\ ἦν\ \text{and} \\ αἱ\ γὰρ\ ἔξοδοί\ μου\ ἔξοδοι\ \underline{ζωῆς} \qquad\qquad\qquad\qquad (\text{viii 35}) \\ ξύλον\ \underline{ζωῆς}\ \dot{\epsilon}στι\ πᾶσι\ τοῖς\ \dot{α}ντεχομ\dot{\epsilon}νοις\ αὐτῆς \qquad (\text{iii 18}) \end{cases}$$

It is clear from the collocation that John uses πρὸς τὸν θεόν for παρὰ τῷ θεῷ, a usage which recurs in the first Epistle in the expression παράκλητον ἔχομεν πρὸς τὸν πατέρα.

This is not to be explained in a mystical manner, as though πρὸς τὸν conveyed some deeper sense than παρὰ τῷ, it means "with God," as commonly translated: the change in grammatical form is due to the writer's or the translator's Greek, or if we prefer it, want of Greek[1], coupled with the fact of the relative paucity of the prepositions in Semitic, which causes the pleonastic representation of a Semitic pronoun by a variety of Greek pronouns, and to some extent the variations of the pronouns *inter se* for persons who do not know much Greek. It is not necessary to assume an actual reference back to the original Hebrew of Proverbs: the Septuagint text will probably be sufficient to explain the form of the Prologue. The restoration of Sophia into the place occupied by the Logos in the Prologue will help us to understand better the course of the argument. For example, the statement that "all

---

[1] Accordingly Euthymius Zigabenus says, πρὸς τὸν θεόν, ἤγουν, παρὰ τῷ πατρί, ἵνα τε παραστήσῃ τὸ ἰδίαζον τῶν ὑποστάσεων καὶ ὅτι ἀχώριστοι πατὴρ καὶ υἱός. On the other hand Liddon, *Bampton Lectures* (p 231), says "He was not merely παρὰ τῷ θεῷ but πρὸς τὸν θεόν This last preposition expresses beyond the fact of co-existence or immanence the more significant fact of perpetuated intercommunion The Face of the Everlasting Word if we dare so to express ourselves, was ever *directed towards* the Face of the Everlasting Father"

things were made by her" is a summary of the verses in Proverbs describing Wisdom's activity at the Creation; while the repetition "and without her nothing was made," shows that we have in the verse a reflection from another passage, where we are told that "in wisdom (or by wisdom) he hath made them *all*" (Ps. civ. 24).

The next step will be to see whether the proposed scheme of evolution for the Johannine Prologue will throw light on the remaining clauses of the argument contained in it. Perhaps, however, this will be sufficient for a first statement So we will merely recapitulate our hypothesis, which is, that the Logos in the Prologue to John is a substitute for Sophia in a previously existing composition, and the language of the Prologue to the Gospel depends ultimately upon the eighth chapter of the Book of Proverbs.

If we are right, then Dr Bridges was right, at least as far as the basal document is concerned, in saying that "in the beginning was *Mind*": for it is *Mind* that is the proper substitute for *Sophia,* and not any particular expression of the rational word, as suggested by Scott Holland in the passage to which we referred at the beginning of this paper

* * * * *

Our hypothesis that the Logos of the Fourth Gospel is a substitute for a previously existing Sophia involves (or almost involves) the consequence that the Prologue is a hymn in honour of Sophia, and that it need not be in that sense due to the same authorship as the Gospel itself The best way to test the hypothesis is to see where it will take us, and what further light it will shed upon the primitive Christian doctrine Let us then retrace our steps for awhile and see whether the foundations of the argument are secure.

The first thing that needs to be emphasised is that we are obliged to take a different view of the Greek of the Fourth Gospel from that which is commonly taken by New Testament exegetes. They are in the habit of describing the Greek of the Gospel as simple, but correct, and of contrasting it in that respect with the Greek of the Apocalypse Our position is that the very first verse of the Gospel ought to have undeceived them as to the linguistic accuracy of the writer, and to have marked him as a "barbarian" in the Greek sense In other words, ἦν πρὸς τὸν θεόν is not Greek at all: and a Greek scholar ought to have felt this at

THE ORIGIN OF THE PROLOGUE TO ST JOHN

the very first reading. The various subtleties which are read into the expression are self-condemned, in that they can neither be justified by the theological thought of the time when the book was composed, nor can they be made to harmonise with the assumed simplicity of the writer's diction When Mr F. A Paley, with the dew of Æschylean studies upon him, and in that sense very far removed from the possibility of understanding Hellenistic Greek, began to translate the oracular opening of the Gospel, he said:

> In the beginning was the Logos, and the Logos was *in relation to God*, and the Logos was God,

and then added a note that "the usual translation 'the Word was with God' (from the Latin Vulgate) conveys no clearly intelligible idea." One wonders what was the clearly intelligible idea that was conveyed by the words "The Logos was in relation to God"!

If Jerome gave us the rendering "apud Deum," he was in any case following the primitive Latin tradition; when the Old Latin version was revised, the original "sermo" was changed to "verbum," but apparently no one thought of changing "apud" into some other preposition What other word ought they to have used if the passage was to remain simple and intelligible? It will not do to lay the burden of unintelligible translation upon the Latin: for even if we assume that the Latin is obscure, we have in the Syriac the rendering—

$$ \text{)ܐܠܗܐ ܠܘܬ} \text{ } (=l_e\text{wath Alaha}) $$

which was, as any Syriac scholar will admit, the only possible rendering of πρὸς τὸν θεόν, and in itself capable of equation with *apud Deum* It is this Syriac rendering that is the key to the understanding of the passage, for (i) it is the equivalent either of πρὸς τὸν θεόν or of παρὰ τῷ θεῷ, and (ii) if we take it in the second of the two senses, we have the exact parallel to the language of the Proverbs, where Wisdom is described as being "with God," in the sense of being seated by God and in attendance upon Him. If the language of the Gospel is to be taken as unintelligible, the language of the Book of Proverbs must be taken as unintelligible also.

Let us, then, leave Mr Paley, who in these matters counts for very little, and let us turn to Dr Westcott, who counts for a very great deal.

8   THE ORIGIN OF THE PROLOGUE TO ST JOHN

The first thing that Westcott says is that "the phrase ($\tilde{\eta}\nu$ $\pi\rho\acute{o}s$, Vulgate *erat apud*) is remarkable. It is found also in Matthew xiii. 56; Mark vi. 3; Mark ix. 19; Mark xiv 49; Luke ix. 41; 1 John i. 2   The idea conveyed by it is not that of simple co-existence, as of two persons contemplated separately in company ($\epsilon\tilde{\iota}\nu\alpha\iota$ $\mu\epsilon\tau\acute{\alpha}$, iii. 26, etc.) or united under a common conception ($\epsilon\tilde{\iota}\nu\alpha\iota$ $\sigma\acute{\upsilon}\nu$, Luke xxii 56) or (so to speak) in local relation ($\epsilon\tilde{\iota}\nu\alpha\iota$ $\pi\alpha\rho\acute{\alpha}$, xvii. 5), but of being (in some sense) *directed towards* and regulated by that with which the relation is fixed (v. 19)"

The passage quoted is characteristically obscure, but we may try to unravel its meaning   Westcott wants to translate $\pi\rho\grave{o}s$ $\tau\grave{o}\nu$ $\theta\epsilon\acute{o}\nu$ as "in the direction of God", so much was due to his pedagogic tradition; but this does not satisfy him, so he prefixes a parenthetic "in some sense" before the words "directed towards," and leaves us to find out as best we may what the sense was in which the Logos was polarised *towards* God   When we come to examine the parallel passages by which the remarkable usage of $\pi\rho\grave{o}s$ is to be justified, we notice that Matthew and Luke ought not to be quoted   Matthew xiii 56 is from Mark vi 3, and Luke ix. 41 is a repetition of Mark ix. 19.   The usage is clearly Marcan; and we have therefore to enquire what Mark meant by saying

    His sisters are with us,

or

    How long shall I be with you ?

or

    I was daily with you in the Temple:

surely the sense of these passages is clear enough: we should not improve the rendering by saying

His sisters are (in some sense) directed towards us and regulated by that which fixes the relation between them and us

The fact that the language is Marcan, taken with the known result of criticism, that Mark's language is, in part at least, Aramaic, encourages us to see how the texts look in the Old Syriac.   The Syriac scholar will know without looking that the equivalent is ܠܘܬ (=l_ewathan) for $\pi\rho\grave{o}s$ $\dot{\eta}\mu\tilde{\alpha}s$ and ܠܘܬܟܘܢ (=l_ewathkōn) for $\pi\rho\grave{o}s$ $\dot{\upsilon}\mu\tilde{\alpha}s$ The Greek then of Mark has carried over a mistranslation of the Syriac ܠܘܬ (l_ewath) exactly similar to what occurs in the Prologue to John   We are dealing with what is called "Translation Greek" or "Semitic Greek." The Marcan and Johannine uses are one and the same. This does not mean that they were incapable of translating the Syriac preposition. St John has the correct παρὰ σεαυτῷ and παρὰ σοί in xvii. 5, where the Syriac reader will note the occurrence of ܠܘܬܟ (l_ewathak) in the Peshito for both expressions (though the older Syriac has a rather cumbrous paraphrase).

[Before leaving the linguistic alley into which we have wandered it will not be waste of time or space to remind readers of New Testament Greek to be on the look-out for usages and misunderstandings similar to the series to which we have been drawing attention. For example, the Aramaic idiom for "he went away" is

ܐܙܠ ܠܗ (ezal leh),

answering very nearly to the Old English "he went him away", the second pronoun in the English and the expletive ܠܗ (= leh, him *or* to him) in Syriac being without an equivalent and untranslatable in modern English. The early translators of the New Testament documents, however, were at pains to find nothing untranslatable and to leave nothing untranslated. For example, in the interpolated passage Luke xxiv. 12, we are told that Peter went away from the tomb in amazement at what had occurred; in Greek it is

ἀπῆλθεν πρὸς αὐτόν

or πρὸς ἑαυτόν,

which evidently stands for a simple Aramaic statement that "Peter went away," and in the first rendering was

ἀπῆλθεν [πρὸς αὐτόν],

where we add brackets to show the redundancy of the translator.

Now we see what happens. The Greek passage goes back into Syriac, the translator does not see that it is a case of his conventional idiom, and laboriously replaces the redundant word by ܠܘܬܗ (l_ewatheh), and so loses the idiom altogether. As we have pointed out, the words πρὸς αὐτόν ought not to have been translated in the first instance, in turning Aramaic discourse into Greek, nor rendered again in the second, in turning a Greek sentence into Syriac.

The whole incident is either derived from the fourth Gospel (John xx. 3–10) or from some closely related document. In the Fourth Gospel, however, we have two disciples visiting the tomb, and not merely Peter: but whether the original story was told of one person or two, it ends up significantly in John with the remark that the two disciples went away πρὸς αὐτούς. This time the Lewis Syriac restores the idiom correctly, ܐܙܠܘ ܠܗܘܢ (ezālu l_ehōn), "they went them away." The Peshito, however, tries to bring more out of the Greek than is really in it, and presents us with "they went away to their 'own' places"]

Now let us return to Sophia. Our supposition that the Logos of the Gospel is a substitute for a primitive Sophia will be confirmed if we can show

(i) that there is any literature, devotional or otherwise, connected with the praises of Sophia:

(ii) if we find that Jesus, who is equated with the Logos, is also equated with the Wisdom of God:

(iii) if the praises of Sophia are as notably derived from the Book of Proverbs, as we have seen the Prologue of the Gospel to be; and

(iv) if the conjunction of Logos and Sophia is intellectually sufficiently close to allow one of them to be interchanged with the other.

With regard to the first and third points, we hardly need to remind ourselves that there is a whole series of Sapiential books, of which the principal representatives, the so-called Wisdom of Solomon, and the Wisdom of Jesus the Son of Sirach, are seen by a very superficial criticism to be pendants to the great hymn in the eighth chapter of Proverbs. If, for example, the Book of Proverbs represents Wisdom as saying,

> I was by Him as one brought up with Him,

this Attendant-Wisdom or Assessor-Wisdom appears in the prayer of Solomon "Give me Wisdom that sits by Thy throne" (Sap. Sol. ix. 4) and is said to have been:

> With thee and aware of thy works, and present with thee at the world's making (Sap Sol ix. 9);

and a further prayer as follows:

> Despatch her from the Holy Heaven,
> Send her from the Throne of Thy Glory
> (Sap. Sol. ix 10);

in all of which passages Wisdom is conceived, as we said before, as the Co-Assessor and Attendant of the Creator. The motive for all these rhythms is in the eighth chapter of Proverbs. The ninth chapter of the Wisdom of Solomon is, in fact, a pendant to the eighth of the Proverbs of Solomon: it occupies an intermediate position between Proverbs and John. More than this, it furnishes the transition from Logos to Sophia, by using parallel language for the two personifications The chapter opens thus·

> O God of our fathers and Lord of Thy mercy,
> Who hast made all things *by Thy Word*,
> And hast ordained man *by Thy Wisdom*

Here the parallel is made between creative word and creative wisdom: the Word and the Wisdom are almost equivalent: the earlier concept, Wisdom, in the Book of Proverbs, by whom all things were made, has attached to it a second concept, the Logos, and what was said of the former is now said of the latter: we have passed from

> Without her was nothing made,

to

> Without Him was nothing made

We have crossed from Proverbs to John; the bridge upon which we crossed is the ninth chapter of the Wisdom of Solomon: so the praises of Sophia become the praises of the Logos

The chapter closes with another suggestive parallelism between Sophia and the Holy Spirit, as follows:

> Who knoweth Thy counsel
> Unless Thou givest Wisdom
> And sendest Thy Holy Spirit from on high?

When we pass from the so-called Wisdom of Solomon to the Wisdom of Jesus the Son of Sirach, we are confronted with similar phenomena to those which we have already adumbrated. Again we see that the underlying text is the Great Chant in Proverbs, and that these so-called Sapiential books are variations of the same theme, that Wisdom is with God, that She is before all things, and that She is involved in the creation of all the works of God.

We are to set over against Proverbs viii 22

> The Lord created me in the beginning of His way,
> Before His works of old,

the passage

> Wisdom has been created before all things,
> Intelligence and understanding from Eternity
> (Sir 1. 4),

and

> The Lord created her Himself,
> *   *   *   *   *
> And shed her forth over all His works
> (Sir. 1. 9)

But when we have made these obvious parallels we cannot detach them from the language of the Prologue:

In the beginning was the Word.
* * * *
All things were made by Him

The dependence of Sirach in its Sophia-doctrine upon Proverbs will be conceded readily enough: whole sentences are, in fact, transferred bodily, e.g :

Proverbs ix 10   ἀρχὴ σοφίας φόβος Κυρίου
Sir   i 14   ἀρχὴ σοφίας φοβεῖσθαι τὸν θεόν

Prov   viii 17   οἱ δὲ ἐμὲ ζητοῦντες εὑρήσουσιν
Sir   iv 11   ἡ σοφία   ἐπιλαμβάνεται τῶν ζητούντων αὐτήν

Prov   viii 36   οἱ μισοῦντές με ἀγαπῶσιν θάνατον
Sir   iv 12   ὁ ἀγαπῶν αὐτὴν ἀγαπᾷ ζωήν

And so on.

It will not, perhaps, be so readily conceded that the language of the Johannine Prologue is a case of similar dependence; the practical difficulty arises from our insufficient familiarity with the language of the Sapiential books, and from the lack of the clue furnished by the inter-relation of σοφία and λόγος, to which we have drawn attention above.

Jesus, then, is identified with the Wisdom of God and the Word of God successively · first with the Wisdom because the Logos-doctrine is originally a Wisdom-doctrine, and after that with the Word, because the Wisdom becomes the Word

It cannot, indeed, be unreasonable to suggest a stage in which Jesus was identified with Wisdom, when, as we have shown, He is called the Wisdom of God by St Paul, who does not present us with the Logos-doctrine, although he does predicate of Christ all that the Fourth Gospel predicates of the Logos   And, as we have shown, the Gospels themselves are in evidence, and perhaps one of the leading Gospel sources (Q) for identifying Christ with the Wisdom of God   The fact is that Logos and Sophia were originally very near together, almost a pair, although under Gnostic speculation they were moved far apart   The substitution of Logos for Sophia in the primitive Christology was little more than the replacing of a feminine expression by a masculine one in Greek-speaking circles, and the transition was very easy   It appears, then, that we can justify the evolution of the Johannine Prologue

THE ORIGIN OF THE PROLOGUE TO ST JOHN 13

from the eighth chapter of Proverbs, and we can show the line of the evolution to have passed through the Sapiential books.

If this be so, we do not need to imitate modern exegetes who speak of the influence of the teaching of Heraclitus upon the Ephesian philosophers or upon the early Ephesian Church It is doubtful whether there is any need to introduce Heraclitus at all. Certainly we can explain further points in the primitive Christology, without turning aside from the path we have already been taking. A Sapiential student, if we may so describe a person who makes himself acquainted, from the Sapiential books, with the virtues and potencies and privileges of the personified Wisdom of God, will tell us, for example, that Wisdom is a *Holy Spirit* and an *Only-Begotten Spirit* (cf Sap Sol vii 22, ἔστιν γὰρ ἐν αὐτῇ πνεῦμα νοερόν, ἅγιον, μονογενές), where, in the first instance, the meaning of the word μονογενής was simply that She was the only one of her kind, a little lower down this expands itself into the statement that "because She is One, She can All" (μία δὲ οὖσα πάντα δύναται [vii 27])

Thus behind the Only-Begotten Son of God to whom John introduces us, we see the Unique Daughter of God, who is His Wisdom, and we ought to understand the Only-Begotten Logos-Son as an evolution from the Only-Begotten Sophia-daughter.

Let us take another instance from the early Christology, not exactly coincident with the Johannine doctrine, but running parallel to it, I mean the Christology of the Epistle to the Hebrews. In the very lofty opening sentences of this Epistle, we find the statement that the Son of God is the heir of all things, and that by Him the ages (or worlds) were made, and that He is the Radiance of the Divine Glory, and the Reflexion of the Divine Being. Now recall what we said of the identification of Jesus with the Wisdom of God, and see what is said in the Wisdom of Solomon of the Divine Wisdom, that she is the

      Radiance[1] of the Eternal Light (vii. 26),
and the
      Spotless Mirror of the Divine Activity,
and the
      Image of His goodness.

The statements from the Epistle to the Hebrews can be deduced at once from the Sapiential books: for it was the Wisdom of God

---
[1] Or perhaps *Reflexion* (ἀπαύγασμα)

14   THE ORIGIN OF THE PROLOGUE TO ST JOHN

that made the worlds, Wisdom that is the Radiance of God (ἀπαύγασμα) and Wisdom that is the imprint of God (χαρακτήρ) in Hebrews, εἰκών and ἔσοπτρον in the Wisdom of Solomon)

Thus we can see the doctrine that Jesus is the Divine Wisdom underlying the Christology of Hebrews.

* * * * *

Now let us come to consider some of the difficulties in the supposed dependence of Logos on Sophia, and of the Johannine Prologue upon Proverbs

Up to the present point, the enquiry can be expressed in the simplest terms The "barbarism" in the opening Greek sentence of the Prologue can almost be made intelligible in English, with Westcott's commentary to help us. and when the peculiar language is corrected, the dependence of the Prologue upon the Book of Proverbs can be established by an English-Bible student, without any outside help The Bible, however, cannot be read satisfactorily apart from the Church History (old Church and new Church) in which it is embedded · and the question at once arises as to whether there is corroborative evidence on the side of the Church History and Literature for the assumed transition from Sophia to Logos: if there is an evolution of the one from the other, why are there no more traces of the change in the Biblical and semi-Biblical literature, and in the writings of the Early Fathers? For it must be admitted that the evidence for Sophia in the New Testament is not overwhelming So we will address ourselves to this point· we want more evidence that Jesus is the Sophia of God, and more evidence that the eighth chapter of Proverbs has been a factor in the production of a primitive Christology

The earliest Christian books, of which we recover traces as having been current in the period that elapsed between the death of the Founder of the Faith and the circulation of the canonical Christian Gospels, are mainly two in number; there was a book called the *Sayings* or *Words of Jesus*, of which fragments occasionally come to light in early papyri or in the citations of early Patristic and other writers, and there was over against this another volume or collection, which comprised *Quotations*, or as they were called *Testimonies*, or with a more explicit title, *Testimonies against the Jews*, the object of which collection of passages from the Jewish writings was to prove to the Jews from the Old

THE ORIGIN OF THE PROLOGUE TO ST JOHN 15

Testament those Christian claims which constitute the doctrine of the New Testament. There need be no doubt as to the antiquity of this anti-Judaic quotation book, for it has survived in a number of more or less modified forms, and its influence may even be detected in the New Testament itself. Amongst the forms in which it has come down to us, one of the most interesting is the three books of *Testimonia adversus Judaeos* which are bound up with the writings of Cyprian: of these the first two are easily seen to be the adaptation by Cyprian of an earlier text-book, which he modifies from time to time, and to which he adds matter which can often be confidently credited to himself. The original arrangement can clearly be made out: the matter is arranged under headings which are almost always primitive, and the selected proof-texts are those which can be traced in the web of not a few early Patristic works.

Now let us look at the second book of Cyprian's *Testimonia*, which contains the Christology, and see how the matter is arranged for the early Jewish objector or enquirer. The book opens with a capitulation as follows:

1. *Christum primogenitum esse et ipsum esse sapientiam Dei*, per quem omnia facta sunt.

2. *Quod Sapientia Dei Christus*, et de sacramento concarnationis eius et passionis et calicis et altaris et Apostolorum[1], qui missi praedicaverunt.

3. Quod Christus idem sit *et sermo Dei*.

4. Quod Christus idem manus et brachium Dei.

And so on.

There is no need to transcribe the rest of the headings under which the citations are grouped. The first two headings appear to stand for a single primitive capitulation, according to which Christ is declared to be the *Wisdom of God*, or, perhaps, the First-born Wisdom of God: and this is followed by a third heading which tells us that the same Christ is the *Logos of God* (*sermo* being the primitive translation of λόγος).

We may say with confidence that the order of appeal made by the early Christian controversialist to the unconverted Jew proceeded from an article which equated Christ with the Wisdom of God, and continued with a proof that the same Christ is the Word of God. The order of the proof is naturally the order of evolution of the Christology. Now let us see how the teaching is presented

[1] The genitives are governed by περί in an original Greek, περὶ μυστηρίου κτέ.

16   THE ORIGIN OF THE PROLOGUE TO ST JOHN

from the Scriptures of the Old Testament. It opens with Proverbs viii. 23–31

> Dominus condidit me initium viarum suarum..
> cum laetaretur orbe perfecto.

Then follows a passage from the Wisdom of Jesus the Son of Sirach, which is introduced as being "from the same Solomon in Ecclesiasticus," the writer having confused the Wisdom of Ben Sira with the so-called Wisdom of Solomon: the passage quoted is xxiv 3–16, 19, and runs as follows (it is necessary to quote the passage in full for there are important consequences that will result from it).

> Ego ex ore Altissimi prodivi ante omnem creaturam
> Ego in caelis feci ut oriretur lumen indeficiens,
> et nebula texi omnem terram
> Ego in altis habitavi et thronus meus in columna nubis.
> Gyrum caeli circumivi et in profundum abyssi penetravi,
> et in fluctibus maris ambulavi et in omni terra steti
> et in omni populo et in omni gente primatum habui
> et omnia excellentium et humilium corda virtute calcavi
> Spes omnis in me vitae et virtutis
> Transite ad me, omnes qui concupiscitis me

The speaker is the Divine Sophia, and the passage in Ben Sira is described as the *Praise of Wisdom* and opens with the statement that "Wisdom will praise herself"

The passage as it stands in the *Testimonies* shows striking variations from the Septuagint and from the Vulgate for example, the opening words in the Greek LXX are

> ἐγὼ ἀπὸ στόματος Ὑψίστου ἐξῆλθον,

and there is nothing to answer to

> ante omnem creaturam

The Vulgate, however, says definitely

> primogenita ante omnem creaturam.

The word *primogenita* is necessary to the argument of the *Testimonies*, which tell us that Christ is the Firstborn and the Wisdom of God And it is still more evident when we notice the coincidence with the language of the Epistle to the Colossians, that "Christ is the firstborn of every creature," which passage is actually quoted a little lower down by the *Testimony Book* It is not necessary to assume, nor is it likely, that the first draft of the *Testimony*

THE ORIGIN OF THE PROLOGUE TO ST JOHN 17

Book quoted New Testament writings at all The point is that Colossians is itself, in part, a book of Testimonies, and that St Paul is quoting from Sirach He has transferred the "Firstborn of every creature" from Sophia to Christ We shall see this more clearly presently Meanwhile observe that the difficulty as to the non-occurrence of the Sophia-doctrine in the New Testament is going to be met It underlies the Pauline Christology as well as the Johannine, and is necessary to its evolution.

The twenty-fourth chapter of Sirach is now seen to be a typical member of a series of *Praises of Wisdom*: but it is equally clear that it is a pendant to the eighth chapter of Proverbs. There can be no doubt as to the origin of the following sentence, when spoken by Sophia:

$$\pi\rho\grave{o} \ \tau o\hat{v} \ a\grave{\iota}\hat{\omega}\nu o s \ \grave{a}\pi' \ \grave{a}\rho\chi\hat{\eta}s \ \check{\epsilon}\kappa\tau\iota\sigma\acute{\epsilon}\nu \ \mu\epsilon$$

Sir xxiv. 9 (14)

Returning to the *Testimony Book*, we note that the second section of the proof that Christ is the Wisdom of God is taken again from Solomon in Proverbs, it is the opening of the ninth chapter of Proverbs · "Wisdom hath builded her house," and is treated as predictive of the Sacraments, but this is a deduction from the equation between Christ and Sophia

The section which follows is the proof that Christ is the Word of God The chief point is to notice that it opens with

Eructavit cor meum verbum bonum (Ps. xlv. 1),

and its appearance in the *Testimony Book* is a sufficient verification of our previous remark that Jerome was not the first to use the Psalm for Christological ends

Assuming then that the equation between Christ and Sophia was fundamental in the *Book of Testimonies*, it will be interesting to take a later form of the same collection, that namely which is attributed to Gregory of Nyssa, and which will be found in the *Collectanea* of Zacagni

Here we shall find many of the Cyprianic Testimonies, but the order of the argument is changed. We begin with the Trinity and with the proof-texts from the Old Testament that Christ is the Word of God. At first sight it looks as if Sophia had disappeared: but as we read on, we suddenly stumble on the expression of 1 Corinthians i. 24, that Christ is the Power of God and the

Wisdom of God. And then follows abruptly something which appears to have been broken away from another setting

> (It says) *in the person of Wisdom, that is to say, of the Son,* when He prepared the Heaven I was there by Him, and I was the One in whom He delighted; every day was I joying before His face.

It is the very passage with which Cyprian opens the second book of his Testimonies to which we referred above.

It is becoming increasingly clear that the eighth chapter of Proverbs, and those associated chapters of the Apocryphal Wisdom-books, are fundamental for the primitive Christology, as it was presented in the proof-texts against Judaism. The *Book of Testimonies*, then, shows clearly that the doctrine that

> Christ is the Word of God

reposes on an earlier doctrine that

> Christ is the Wisdom of God.

The Prologue to the Fourth Gospel is constructed out of the material furnished by the *Praises of Wisdom*, and the very same material is seen to underlie the great Christological passage in the Epistle to the Colossians. In both of these great passages we have to translate the language back into an earlier and intermediate form. For instance, it will have struck the reader of the *Praise of Wisdom* in the twenty-fourth chapter of Sirach that the expression

> In every people and in every race I had the primacy (*primatum habui*)

is something like the expression in Colossians, "that in all things he might have the pre-eminence"; and Cyprian (or one of his forbears) thought so too, for he follows his identification of the Firstborn Wisdom with "Christ the firstborn of every creature" (Col. i. 15), and adds the remark: "Item illic: primogenitus a mortuis ut fieret in omnibus ipse primatum tenens."

In the Greek the identification is not quite so easy: the text of Sirach is often faulty: as commonly edited we have the sentence

> ἐν παντὶ λαῷ καὶ ἔθνει ἐκτησάμην (Sir xxiv. 6)

which has probably to be corrected to ἡγησάμην; for this there is MS. authority, which would answer exactly to *primatum habui*, and we may then discuss whether this is not also a proper equivalent of πρωτεύων in the Epistle to the Colossians.

THE ORIGIN OF THE PROLOGUE TO ST JOHN 19

In any case, we have to go over the Christological passage in Colossians, and underline as probably Sapiential such terms as

εἰκὼν τοῦ Θεοῦ τοῦ ἀοράτου
πρωτότοκος πάσης κτίσεως
ἐν αὐτῷ ἐκτίσθη τὰ πάντα
τὰ πάντα δι' αὐτοῦ .ἔκτισται
ὅς ἐστιν ἀρχή

and ἐν πᾶσιν αὐτὸς πρωτεύων

II

In the previous section we examined the primitive books of *Testimonies against the Jews*, in order to see whether they showed any traces of an evolution of the Logos-Christology out of a previous Sophia-Christology. The results were significant, and we were able to take the further step of affirming that the great Christological passage in the Epistle to the Colossians was like the Prologue to the Fourth Gospel in its ultimate dependence upon the eighth chapter of Proverbs. The next step would seem to be an enquiry as to whether these results are confirmed by Patristic study. Do the early Christian Fathers show, by survival or reminiscence, or in any other way, any traces of (*a*) the equation between Christ and Sophia, or (*b*) any signs that the famous statement that "the Lord created me the beginning of His way, before His works of old," has been a factor that can be recognised in the development of the doctrine of the Person of Christ. To these points we may now address ourselves. In so doing, we may occasionally be repeating the evidence of the previous section, for the reason that the earliest Patristic literature is coloured by the conventional *Testimonies* that were employed by Christian propagandists; but this overlapping is inevitable, and we need not discount the evidence of Irenaeus or Justin because it contains elements that run parallel to the *Book of Testimonies*. if they are saying the same things twice over, in any case, they say them from a different point of view, and by the mouth of fresh witnesses. Justin Martyr, for example, uses the method of prophetic testimony beyond any other Christian writer; but his evidence runs far beyond the small pocket edition of Quotations used by a primitive controversialist. Let us leave the hypothetical *Book of Testimonies*, and if we please, the actual Cyprianic collection, and ask

2—2

the question whether Justin ever calls Christ Sophia, and whether he argues from the Sapiential books when he develops his Christology.

Here is a striking passage from the *Dialogue with Trypho* (c. 139), where Justin has been deducing plurality in the Godhead from the book of Genesis ("Behold, the man has become one of us" and similar well-known passages), and where he goes on to quote Proverbs, under the title of Sophia, as though the real Wisdom of Solomon was the book of Proverbs itself. So he says:

"In Sophia it is said: If I announce to you everyday occurrences I can also recall matters out of eternity. The Lord created me the beginning of his ways.... Before the hills He begat me"

After quoting the famous speech of Sophia from the Book of Sophia, he turns to his listeners and says that the thing which is here said to be begotten is declared by the Word of God to have been begotten before all created things, and every one will admit that there is a numerical distinction between that which begets and that which is begotten We see that Justin uses the word Logos, not for Christ but for the Scripture, the Heavenly Birth is not the Logos but the Divine Wisdom, which he identifies with Christ. In a previous chapter (c 126) he definitely calls Christ the Wisdom of God, after the manner of the *Book of Testimonies*, to which he may even be referring, and he says: "Who can this be who is sometimes called the Angel of the Great Counsel, and by Ezekiel is called a man, and by Daniel like a Son of Man, and by Isaiah a child, and Christ and God worshipful by David, and Christ and a Stone by many writers, and *Sophia by Solomon*, etc , etc."

In the sixty-first chapter of the same dialogue, Justin goes over the same ground, and introduces the matter as follows

"I am now going to give you, my friends, another Testimony from the Scriptures that God before all His other creatures begat as the Beginning a certain spiritual Power, which is also called Glory by the Holy Spirit, and sometimes Son, *and sometimes Sophia*, and sometimes Angel, and sometimes God, and *sometimes Lord and Word*, and sometimes calls himself Commander-in-Chief, etc." He then continues that "The Word of Wisdom will attest what I say, being itself God begotten from the Father of the Universe, and being *Word and Wisdom* and the Glory of its Sire, as Solomon affirms": after which we are again treated to Proverbs viii 21–36. It is clear that this speech of Sophia in the eighth of Proverbs occupied a large space in the accumulated material for Justin's Christology.

Now let us turn to the writings of Theophilus of Antioch whose three books addressed to Autolycus are dated in 168 A.D. We shall find in Theophilus the two streams of Christology flowing into one another, and we can actually see the absorption of the doctrine that

Christ is the Wisdom of God,

by the doctrine that

Christ is the Logos of God.

For awhile they flow side by side, but it needs no commentator to point out which of the two is to absorb the other. For instance, when Theophilus talks of the Creation of the world, he tells us:

Ps xxxiii 6. God by His Word and His Wisdom made all things: for by His Word were the Heavens established, and all their host by His Spirit. Very excellent is His Wisdom.

Prov. iii 19: By Wisdom God founded the earth, and He prepared the Heavens by understanding. Theoph *ad Autol* 1. 7

He returns to the theme at a later point where his language will require careful consideration

Ps xlv. 1. God having within Himself His own inherent Word, begat Him with His own Wisdom, having emitted Him before the Universe.

This passage is, for our purpose, important, (1) for the co-existence of the Word of God and the Wisdom of God[1], (2) because the word *emitted* ($\dot{\epsilon}\xi\epsilon\rho\epsilon\upsilon\xi\acute{a}\mu\epsilon\nu o\varsigma$) is due to the finding of the "good word" in Ps. xlv (My heart is emitting a good word). this identification of the Logos with the language of the psalm we have shown to be very early, and to have been current in the primitive *Book of Testimonies*. Theophilus goes on. This Word He had as His assistant in the things that were made by Him, and it was through Him that He made all things. This "Word" is called beginning ($\dot{a}\rho\chi\acute{\eta}$) because he is ruler ($\check{a}\rho\chi\epsilon\iota$) and lord of all things that have

---

[1] Athanasius frequently restates this equation, which is a commonplace with him *e g ἐν ταύτῃ γὰρ καὶ τὰ πάντα γέγονεν, ὡς ψάλλει Δαβίδ, Πάντα ἐν Σοφίᾳ ἐποίησας καὶ Σολομών φησὶν Ὁ Θεὸς τῇ Σοφίᾳ ἐθεμελίωσε τὴν γῆν, ἠτοίμασε δὲ οὐρανοὺς ἐν φρονήσει Αὐτὴ δὲ ἡ Σοφία ἐστιν ὁ Λόγος, καὶ δι' αὐτοῦ, ὡς Ἰωάννης φησίν, Ἐγένετο τὰ πάντα κτέ* Orat I contra Arianos 19

Note the connexion with the Prologue

been created by Him. It was He, who, being the Spirit of God, and the Beginning and the Wisdom and Power of the Most High, descended on the prophets and through them discoursed of the Creation of the World and all other matters. Not that the prophets were themselves at the Creation of the World; but what was present was the Wisdom of God that was in it (the World?) and the Holy Word of His that was always with Him.

Here we see that the reference to the Logos as Beginning (ἀρχή) leads at once to the introduction of the Sophia who is the Archē of the O.T. The writer says as much: the Logos is Archē and Wisdom. When he states the co-existence of the Word and the Wisdom in Creation, he uses of the Logos the expression "always present with Him" (ἀεὶ συμπαρὼν αὐτῷ) which we recognise at once as borrowed from the description of Wisdom in the eighth chapter of Proverbs. And lest we should miss the reference, and the consequent equivalence of Word and Wisdom, Theophilus explains:

> This is why He speaks as follows through Solomon
> When He prepared the heavens I was by Him,
> (συμπαρήμην αὐτῷ), etc. Theoph. *ad Autol* ii. 10.

The Logos-doctrine of Theophilus, then, although earlier than himself (as is clear not only from his well-known references to the opening verses of John, but also from the use of Ps. xlv), is based upon a still earlier Wisdom-doctrine, which it is gradually displacing.

Sophia does not, however, wholly disappear; Theophilus goes on to talk of the creation of Light and the Luminaries, and explains that "the three days which elapsed before the creation of the Luminaries, are a type of the Trinity, i e of God, and *His Word and his Wisdom.*" This is the first mention of the Trinity in theological literature, in express terms (τριάς), and Theophilus arrives at it by a bifurcation of the original Wisdom into Word and Wisdom, the τριάς being thus an evolution of a previous δυάς: if we prefer to put it so, we may say that Theophilus identified the Wisdom-Christ, now detached from the Logos-Christ, with the Holy Spirit. It will be seen from the foregoing that theologians will have to make a new study of the doctrine of Christ the Wisdom of God, and that incidentally, the often quoted passages in Theophilus will obtain a fresh illumination. For it is no casual remark that Theophilus has dropped; it expresses his fundamental

THE ORIGIN OF THE PROLOGUE TO ST JOHN 23

position: he returns to it later, when he has to explain the plurality of the language in Genesis ("Let us make man");

> To no one else did he say, Let us make man, but to *His own Logos and His own Sophia* (II 18);

and again, when he has to explain how God could appear in a garden and converse with man, he says:

> It was *His Word*, by whom He made all things, *which was His Power and His Wisdom*, that assumed the Person of the Father and Lord of the Universe, and so came into the garden, etc. (II. 22).

The foregoing passages will suffice to show the direction in which Christian thought was moving and what it was moving into

Next let us turn to Irenaeus. We shall find that the matter is now complicated by the Gnostic theories about the aeon Sophia, who has gone astray, and is not the Redeemer, but the lost one to be redeemed

In the following passage, Irenaeus undertakes to prove the Eternal Sonship by a quotation, he says, "We have abundantly shown that the Logos, that is, the Son, was always with the Father, and he says through Solomon, that Sophia also, who is the Spirit, was with Him before any created thing. For "the Lord by Wisdom established the Earth, by understanding He created the Heaven By His knowledge the depths were broken up, and the clouds drop down dew" (Prov. III 19, 20) And again. "the Lord created me the beginning of His way," and so on, Proverbs VIII. 22–25 Here we see Irenaeus (lib. IV. c. 34, § 2, p. 253 Massuet) using the very same passage from the speech of Wisdom concerning herself, and applying it to the Holy Spirit. It is clear that the Sophia-doctrine is one of the oldest pieces of Christology that we can detect, and that it precedes and underlies the doctrine of the Christ and the doctrine of the Holy Spirit.

When Irenaeus has finished his quotation from Proverbs, he continues.

> So there is one God, who *by His Word and His Wisdom* has made all things;

in which we again see the collocation of Sophia and Logos, and infer the replacement of one of them by the other, in accordance with our hypothesis

Nor should it escape our notice, in view of what we detected in the Cyprianic Testimonies of the transfer of the Pre-eminence of Sophia to the Pre-eminence of Christ, that the very same thing is said by Irenaeus which was disclosed by Cyprian   In the chapter which precedes the one from which we were just quoting, we find the following sequence·

Omnia Verbo fecit et Sapientia adornavit, accipiens omnium potestatem, quando Verbum caro factum est, ut quemadmodum in caelis principatum habuit Verbum Dei, sic et in terra haberet principatum,   principatum autem habeat eorum quae sunt sub terra, ipse primogenitus mortuorum factus.

Here again we see that the passage in Colossians (i 18) depends upon the twenty-fourth chapter of Sirach, which is used in the *Testimonies* to prove that Christ is the Wisdom of God. The groundwork of Irenaeus' argument is that "Wisdom has made the world and holds the primacy in it": but this he expands by coupling Logos with Sophia in the opening sentence, and by substituting Logos for Sophia in the language borrowed from Sirach. The evolution of the Christology can be made out with sufficient clearness. The Logos is first substituted for Sophia, and then in the Wisdom passages the Word and the Wisdom appear together

*   *   *   *   *   *

III

The same enquiry can be made in other writers of the same period, Tertullian, for example   In writing against Praxeas, whose Sabellianism was to be confuted, it became necessary for Tertullian to re-state the doctrine of the Trinity in such a way as to preclude the "Crucifixion of the Father"

He tells us to listen to Sophia as a second created person. Then follows the famous passage in Proverbs. "The Lord created me the Beginning," and he explains that Sophia is a constituent of Logos.   He then points out it is the Son in His own person who *under the name of Sophia* confesses the Father   For though in the passage quoted it might seem as if Sophia were herself created by the Lord for His works and His ways, *yet we must remember that elsewhere it is said that all things were made by the Logos, and nothing made without Him*   Tertullian accordingly replaces Sophia by Logos in the passage from the eighth of Proverbs, and this proves that the Logos is not the Father   It is easy to infer that the displacing Logos is itself a derivative from that which it displaces. At all events, Tertullian saw clearly the interdependence of the Wisdom passage and the Prologue They cannot be kept apart

Much more is said by Tertullian on the relation of the Divine Wisdom to the Divine Word in his tract against Hermogenes, who would have the universe created out of previously existing matter. Tertullian denies the existence of this uncreate matter "the apostles and prophets did not thus explain the creation of the world by the mere appearance of God and His approach to existing matter, they never mention matter at all, but *first of all they say that Sophia was created the Beginning of His ways for His works*, as in the eighth chapter of Proverbs, and *after that came the emitted Word* by whom all things were made and nothing made without Him.

Here we see the same collocation of the Sophia story and the Logos Prologue, and that Sophia has a certain priority to the Logos

It is not necessary to deal with the matter at greater length in this connexion All students of Theology and of Church History know that the Wisdom passages in Proverbs became the standard proof-texts for the doctrine of the Eternal Sonship, and that around the words "The Lord created me," etc., raged the battle with the Arians, who, like their antagonists, regarded the Greek text with its ἔκτισεν for ἐκτήσατο as sacrosanct All that we have to do is to note the theological interdependence of the eighth of Proverbs and the Johannine Prologue, and to emphasise that one of them is, by admitted consanguinity, derived from the other.

It may be interesting to find out whether Origen has anything to say on the collocations which we have made and the inferences which we have drawn We shall find that, like the earlier Fathers and the authors of the Testimony books, he identifies the Logos with the *Eructatio* of the forty-fourth Psalm, and then finds himself in the difficulty that the Psalm continues with *Audi filia* How could the Logos be addressed in the feminine? His explanation is that such changes of persons are common, we have to remember that the Logos was in the Beginning, but it is conceded from the Testimonies in the Proverbs that Sophia is the Beginning, for "the Lord created me the Beginning, etc"; and this makes Sophia a prior concept to Logos which expresses it Hence the

Evangelist does not merely say that the Logos was with God, but that the Logos was in the Beginning (sc in Sophia) with God.

There is much more of the same in the Commentary of Origen upon John, but this will suffice to show that Origen also has clearly before him the connexion between the Prologue and Proverbs, and that he holds, in a certain sense, the subordination of Logos to Sophia (See Origen *in Joann.* lib. I cc. 34, 39, etc)[1]

The chain of Patristic interpretation which deduces Logos from Sophia is practically unbroken: the finding of the investigation may be summed up in the *Prophetic Eclogues* of Eusebius (pp. 98 sqq.), who tells that the whole of the Book of Proverbs appears to be written in the person of Wisdom, who sometimes lays down ethical principles, and sometimes takes to herself the words of others: at one time offering us riddles, and at another teaching us concerning herself and instructing us as to her own Divine dignity From these we may select whereby to learn that Wisdom is indeed a Divine creature and altogether to be praised in her nature, being the same as the second cause of the Universe after the prime Deity, and as the Word-God who was in the beginning with God, and as the Providence of God which regulates and orders all things, and penetrates to matters terrestrial, which Wisdom was created before every other Being and Substance, being the Beginning of the Ways of the whole creation And what she, Sophia, says herself is on this wise Then follows Proverbs viii 12: This, then, is the teaching of Wisdom concerning herself, and who she is the holy Apostle teaches us, saying:

> Christ the power of God and the Wisdom of God (1 Cor i. 24)

And again

> Who of God is made unto us Wisdom (1 Cor. i 30)

It is Christ, then, who is the speaker in the passage from Proverbs Wisdom is also the Word of God, by whom all things are made For "In the beginning was the Word and the Word was with God, and the Word was God. All things were made by Him," and

> By Him were all things created, whether in Heaven or on Earth, whether visible or invisible, as the Apostle says (Col i 16)

[1] Πάλιν δὲ ἀρχὴ καὶ τέλος ὁ αὐτός ἀλλ' οὐ κατὰ τὰς ἐπινοίας ὁ αὐτός ἀρχὴ γάρ, ὡς ἐν ταῖς παροιμίαις μεμαθήκαμεν, καθὸ σοφία τυγχάνει, ἐστί γέγραπται γοῦν Ὁ Θεὸς ἔκτισέ με ἀρχὴν ὁδῶν αὐτοῦ εἰς τὰ ἔργα αὐτοῦ καθὸ δὲ λόγος ἐστίν, οὐκ ἔστιν ἀρχή ἐν ἀρχῇ γὰρ ἦν ὁ λόγος.

THE ORIGIN OF THE PROLOGUE TO ST JOHN 27

And just as in one aspect He is called the Word of God, and in another Life and Truth and True Light, and whatever other names the Scriptures give Him, *so also He is entitled Sophia*, the Handmaid of the Father for the Providence and Regulation of the Universe

In these words Eusebius hands on the ecclesiastical traditions which we have been considering, identifying Sophia and Logos, and explaining the Prologue in John and the Christological passage in Colossians by the help of the eighth chapter of Proverbs, from which they are thus admitted to have been derived

It is not for the sake of multiplying references that we cite one Father after another, but with the object of showing the continuity and consistency of the Patristic tradition, which appears to have been inadequately treated by leading commentators of our day, who did not see the meaning of the constant reference to Christ as the Wisdom of God, nor recognise the close connexion between these early Patristic commentaries and the primitive collections of Testimonies To illustrate the matter once more from a fresh point of view, suppose we go back to the opening capitulations of the second book of Cyprian's *Testimonies*, the book that contains the prophecies concerning Jesus Christ. We pointed out that these opening summaries of the sections that are to follow bore evidence of having been somewhat modified, for example, that the theme of the first chapter was originally the identification of Christ with the Wisdom of God, and that this Wisdom was the firstborn (primogenita), the adjective being applied to Sophia in the first instance Now if we were to turn to Eusebius, *Evangelical Demonstration*, we should find the very same theme before us, the collection of prophetic arguments for Christological purposes, and it would be quite easy to show that Eusebius, while working with great freedom, is not independent of the approved Testimonies which have come down from the early days of the Church

The first chapter of the fifth book of the *Demonstratio Evangelica* has for its heading the statement that "among the Hebrews the most wise Solomon was aware of a certain *firstborn* ($\pi\rho\omega\tau\acute{o}\tau o\kappa os$) Power of God, which he also entitles His Wisdom and His Offspring, with the same honour that we ourselves also bestow." Compare that with the Firstborn Wisdom of the Testimonies, and then note how the writer plunges at once into Proverbs viii., and after enumerating the praises of Wisdom, remarks that

28 THE ORIGIN OF THE PROLOGUE TO ST JOHN

Wisdom is the Divine and all-virtuous Substance that precedes all created things, the intellectual (νοερός) and firstborn (πρωτότοκος) Image (εἰκών) of the Unbegotten Nature, the true-born and only-born (μονογενής) Son of the God of all.

Here Christ is declared to be the Wisdom of God, in *the terms in which Wisdom is described in Proverbs and the other Sapiential Books* (see especially Sap. Sol vii 22 sqq) And, just as in the early Testimonies, Eusebius goes on to quote Colossians (i. 15, 17) and complete the proof that Christ is the Firstborn of every Creature; for Christ, he says, was speaking in His own person when Wisdom (apparently) spoke in hers The equation between Christ and the Wisdom of God covers the whole of the argument

Reviewing the course of the enquiry, we see that the commentators upon the great Christological passages in the New Testament, the Prologue to St John, and the parallel passage in Colossians, have failed to set these passages in the true line of their historical evolution We have tried to restate the texts upon which the accepted Christology is based, first by correcting a grammatical error in the first verse of St John's Gospel, which ought to have been obvious to an unsophisticated reader; second, by showing that the theology of the Church is best seen in the first days of its making by a careful consideration of the primitive books of Testimonies, it follows from these corrections and identifications that the key to the language of the Johannine Prologue and to St Paul's language in the Epistle to the Colossians lies in the Sapiential tradition, and not in the reaction from Plato or Philo or Heraclitus.

It is not pretended that this point of view is altogether new. Many critics and interpreters have occasionally come near to it; few have altogether ignored it, but it is not sufficient to put a stray marginal reference to Proverbs or Sirach in the New Testament, we must examine those occasional references and disclose the system to which they belong It will perhaps surprise some students to know that it was Alford who came nearest to what we believe to be the right solution at least, the following sentences from his commentary are significant for the identification of the Word of God and the Wisdom of God ·

" We are now to enquire how it came that St John found this *word* λόγος *so ready made to his hands, as to require no explanation* The answer to this will be found by tracing the *gradual personifica-*

THE ORIGIN OF THE PROLOGUE TO ST JOHN 29

tion of the *Word* or *Wisdom of God*, in the Old Testament .. As the *Word* of God was the constant idea for his revelations *relatively to man*, so was the *Wisdom* of God for those which related to *His own essence* and attributes That this was a later form of expression than the simple recognition of the Divine Word in the Mosaic and early historical books, would naturally be the case ... In Sap Sir ı 1 Wisdom is said to be

$$\pi\alpha\rho\grave{\alpha}\ \mathrm{K}\upsilon\rho\acute{\iota}o\upsilon\ \kappa\alpha\grave{\iota}\ \mu\epsilon\tau'\ a\mathring{\upsilon}\tau o\mathring{\upsilon}\ \epsilon\mathring{\iota}s\ \tau\grave{\upsilon}\nu\ a\mathring{\iota}\hat{\omega}\nu\alpha$$

Then in c xxiv. 9, 21, the same strain is continued,

$$\pi\rho\grave{o}\ \tau o\hat{\upsilon}\ a\mathring{\iota}\hat{\omega}\nu o s\ \mathring{a}\pi'\ \mathring{a}\rho\chi\eta s\ \mathring{\epsilon}\kappa\tau\iota\sigma\acute{\epsilon}\nu\ \mu\epsilon$$

In the Book of the Wisdom of Solomon we find a similar personification and eulogy of Wisdom In this remarkable passage we have Wisdom called

$$\pi\acute{\alpha}\rho\epsilon\delta\rho o s\ \tau\hat{\omega}\nu\ \sigma\hat{\omega}\nu\ \theta\rho\acute{o}\nu\omega\nu\ (\text{c ix 4}),$$

and said to have been

$$\pi\alpha\rho o\hat{\upsilon}\sigma\alpha\ \mathring{o}\tau\epsilon\ \mathring{\epsilon}\pi o\acute{\iota}\epsilon\iota s\ \tau\grave{\upsilon}\nu\ \kappa\acute{o}\sigma\mu o\nu,$$

and parallelised with

$$\mathring{o}\ \lambda\acute{o}\gamma o s\ \sigma o\upsilon\ (\text{c ix 12, c xvi 12})\ ''$$

The foregoing passages indicate the right way to approach the subject, and are only in error in the assumption that the Sophia of the Old Testament is a later development of the Logos.

If we are substantially right in the foregoing investigation, the next step will be to see how much further elucidation of St John's Prologue will result from the restoration of Sophia to its right place in the theme This further enquiry will involve important considerations

Before, however, we turn to this part of the enquiry it will be interesting to show that the suggestion of hymns in honour of Sophia, produced in the time that is adjacent to that in which the Fourth Gospel was written, is not a hypothesis destitute of illustration outside of the Scriptures We actually have a Sophia-hymn of the kind that we have described in the *Odes of Solomon*.

The twenty-third Ode of this collection, after a somewhat obscure opening, in which Divine Grace appears to be speaking in the Person of Christ, goes on to tell of a Perfect Virgin, who stands and cries to men ·

"There stood a perfect Virgin, who was proclaiming and calling and saying, O ye sons of men, return ye, O ye daughters, come ye: and forsake the ways of that corruption and draw near unto me, and I will enter into you and will bring you forth from perdition, and make you wise in the ways of truth, that you be not destroyed nor perish· hear ye me, and be redeemed. For the Grace of God I am telling among you, and by my means you shall be redeemed and become blessed I am your judge; and they who have put me on shall not be injured; but they shall possess immortality in the new world: my chosen ones, walk ye in me, and my ways will I make known to them that seek me, and I will make them trust in my name."

One has only to recall the language of the Book of Proverbs in the beginning of the eighth chapter,

> Doth not Wisdom cry?
> And Understanding put forth her voice?
> * * * * *
> Unto you, O men, I call;
> And my voice is to the sons of men

It is clear that the Virgin speaker is *Sophia* and we are to illustrate the Ode in question by Proverbs viii, upon which it is based. It will be easy to adduce fresh parallels to the language, but what is really important for us to note is that the Sophia who speaks exchanged personality with the Christ "I will make them trust in my name"; and the "Grace who stands on a lofty summit" (at the beginning of the Ode) and cries from one end of the earth to the other, is, perhaps, only a modification of the figure of Wisdom in Proverbs viii. 2, who "standeth on the top of high places"

Thus we have actually found a Sophia-Christ-Ode in the early Christian Church, quite unconnected with the Sophia that we discovered in the *Testimony Book* Note in passing that she describes herself as a Preacher of Divine Grace

In the preceding series of arguments we have attempted to show that St John in his Prologue was working from existing materials, which comprise the *Praises of Sophia* in the Sapiential Books, and perhaps from some Sophia-songs that are no longer extant There are foundations apparent underneath his edifice, and it is only reasonable to ask whether we can go further in the detection of the sources, and whether we can thereby throw any further light upon the language of the Prologue

For example, we have in the seventh chapter of the book of Wisdom, a description of Wisdom as the Radiance of the Eternal

THE ORIGIN OF THE PROLOGUE TO ST JOHN

Light, and it is natural to compare this with the Johannine doctrine that Christ is the Light, and the doctrine of the Epistle to the Hebrews that Christ is the Radiance of the Father's Glory. When we read a little further we find (Sap Sol. vii 29) that Sophia is "more illustrious than the Sun and brighter than the positions of all stars," and that compared with all "created" Light (*or* with "day"-light) she is found to be anterior;

φωτὶ συγκρινομένη εὑρίσκεται προτέρα

this answers very well to the statement in the Fourth Gospel that "in Him was Life and the Life was the Light of men", we may imagine, if we please, an earlier form that

In her was Life, and the Life was the Light of men:

or

In her was Light and the Light was the Life of men;

but now see what follows: the writer goes on to argue for the priority and the permanence of the Light in these words:

Night, indeed, follows on created Light,
But no evil overpowers <i>Wisdom</i>[1].</div>

Here we evidently have the origin of the phrase in the Johannine Prologue, which is commonly rendered,

and the darkness comprehended it not:

but which is better expressed in Moffatt's translation,

Amid the darkness the Light shone,
But the darkness did not master it

There can hardly be a reasonable doubt that the explanation of the phrase in John is to be found in the passage of the Wisdom of Solomon It does not require any philosophical reference to dualistic conflicts between Good and Evil, and Light and Darkness, *except as such conflicts are assumed in the language of the Wisdom of Solomon* The darkness which masters the light is the darkness which comes on at the end of the day, existing potentially throughout the day but operating triumphantly when the end of the day comes We are to take κατέλαβεν in John i 5 as the equivalent of ἀντισχύει in Sap Sol vii 30, and to say that Wisdom, being the Radiance of the Everlasting Light, has no ending to the day which it produces. Thus the chapter which furnished us with the explanation of the Johannine *Only-Begotten*, the *Radiance* of

---

[1] The corresponding sentence in Proverbs appears to be iii. 15 οὐκ ἀντιτάξεται αὐτῇ (sc σοφίᾳ) οὐδὲν πονηρόν.

Hebrews, and the *Image* in Colossians, furnishes us also with the clue to the argument in John 1 5, and with the right way to translate the words

Our next instance shall be the great Incarnation verse (John 1. 14), which tells us that

> The Word became flesh and dwelt among us·

where there is much discussion as to the meaning of the word ἐσκήνωσεν, which is connected by etymology with the word σκηνή (a tabernacle or tent) and so with the Hebrew word *Shekinah*. Moffatt, indeed, discards this explanation, perhaps as being too subtle and mystical, and tells us to translate,

> So the Logos became flesh and tarried among us.

and the first impulse of an educated theologian would be to annotate the rendering as inadequate. Yet Alford says "*sojourned* or *tabernacled* the word is one technically used in Scripture to import the *dwelling of God among men*". and there is not much difference between "sojourned" of Alford and "tarried" of Moffatt Since, however, we are arguing from the hypothesis that the Logos has been evolved from Sophia, the first thing to be done is to ask whether σκηνόω or its equivalent κατασκηνόω is one of the Sapiential words, and in what sense it is used in the *Praises of Wisdom* The answer is that it occurs over and over again in the Αἴνεσις Σοφίας in the twenty-fourth chapter of Sirach: for example

Sir. xxiv 4. I dwelt (κατεσκήνωσα) on high
* * * * *
Sir xxiv. 8. He that created me pitched *my tent* (σκηνήν),
And said, *Dwell thou* in Jacob (κατασκήνωσον)
Let thy inheritance be in Israel.
(= Prov viii. 22). Before the world from the Beginning He created me,
(And said) unto the end of the world I will not forsake thee.
In the Holy Tabernacle (σκηνῇ) before Him I ministered,
And thus was I established in Zion:
In the beloved City likewise He made me to rest,
And in Jerusalem was my authority:
I took root among the honoured people,
In the Lord's portion of His inheritance

Reading these rhythms carefully we see they are founded on the eighth chapter of Proverbs, and that they essay to prove that Wisdom has made her dwelling among the Jews, and especially in Jerusalem He says this over and over in eight different ways

THE ORIGIN OF THE PROLOGUE TO ST JOHN

and he uses the etymology of σκηνόω from σκηνή and suggests that we may have to employ the awkward word *Tabernacle* instead of *dwelling* or *tarriance* if we are to bring out the force of his words. It results, moreover, from these Sapiential passages, which lead up to the *Dwelling* or *Tabernacling* of the Logos, that we ought to understand in John i 14 that the Logos made His dwelling among the Jews, and in this case we must look back a sentence or two, and understand the words "He came to His own, and His own received Him not," in the sense that "He came to the Jews," and here we shall be again surprised to find Alford saying: "τὰ ἴδια cannot well mean *the world*, or οἱ ἴδιοι *mankind in general*: it would be difficult to point out any Scripture usage to justify such a meaning But abundance of passages bear out the meaning which makes τὰ ἴδια his own inheritance or possession, i e Judaea; and οἱ ἴδιοι the Jews. compare especially the parable Matthew xxi 33 ff and Sirach xxiv 7 ff " Here Alford actually quotes from the *Praises of Wisdom*, only beginning at an earlier point with the words,

<blockquote>With all this I sought for rest,
And in whose inheritance shall I make my dwelling ?"</blockquote>

Nor is it less interesting that Westcott makes the very same explanation and quotes the very same passage· what they both appear to miss is that the references (which are more to the point than they imagined) carry with them the sense of ἐσκήνωσεν in John i. 14, and that, therefore, if, as Westcott supposes, ἐσκήνωσεν ἐν ἡμῖν refers to the indwelling of Christ in believers, and not to anything of a racial character, it can only carry this meaning as an antithesis to the known dwelling of Sophia amongst the Jews in Jerusalem It is, however, doubtful if we ought to resort to antithesis. The first draft of the argument appears to have been of the type that

<blockquote>In Jewry God is known,</blockquote>

and the first persons who received the Messiah are of the group described as οἱ ἴδιοι, i e of the Jews Naturally we go on to refer to such believing Jews the words,

<blockquote>The Sophia-Logos dwelt among us</blockquote>

It will now be clear that this investigation divides itself into two parts, (1) the discovery of those Johannine and Colossian terms which belong to the Sapiential tradition; (2) the enquiry whether in either John or Colossians an additional Sapiential document should be assumed to underlie the Christian teaching A good deal has been done in the way of defining which terms are really Sapiential: we can underline ἀρχή and ἀπαύγασμα and εἰκών and ἐσκήνωσεν and πρωτότοκος and μονογενής, as well as certain sentences in which the action of the Divine Wisdom is intimated. Some of these sentences do not require a special bridge to be built for them from the Sapiential books to the New Testament: the statements

and
πάντα δι' αὐτοῦ ἐγένετο (John 1 3),

ἐν αὐτῷ ἐκτίσθη τὰ πάντα (Col 1 16),

are equivalents to the language of Proverbs, which are capable of immediate deduction, so soon as we have agreed that Jesus is the Wisdom of God So also the doctrine that

αὐτός ἐστιν πρὸ πάντων (Col 1 17)

is an immediate consequence of the existence of Sophia πρὸ τοῦ αἰῶνος, and similarly for other obvious deductions It is not so easy, however, to infer the immediate derivation of such terms as Μονογενής or Πρωτότοκος. No doubt Monogenēs is a Sapiential term, but it is as unique in use as it is in meaning When we come to the Gospel we find that it is one of the current words of the New Testament religion, and it is difficult to believe that it acquired currency so immediately, as to become, by one stroke, from an obscure adjective, one of the leading terms of theology. We seem to need an intermediate document, but do not quite see how to prove that it is absolutely required To suspect is not enough

Meanwhile, it is interesting to observe that Colossians does not exactly agree with St John in its treatment of the Logos-theme. In Colossians 1 18 Jesus is the ἀρχή in agreement with Proverbs,

ἀρχὴν ἔκτισέν με

But in John this is somewhat obscured, and the language of Proverbs is interpreted to mean ἐν ἀρχῇ . the source is the same, the treatment is different. In Colossians, Jesus is the Firstborn who has the First Rank, even among the dead. We have shown reason to suspect that this is an interpretation of a primitive ἡγήσατο, used of the Firstborn taking the lead; but in the Gospel we have what looks like a variant of the same theme, viz,

THE ORIGIN OF THE PROLOGUE TO ST JOHN

"Μονογενής ἐκεῖνος ἐξηγήσατο," where the difficulty of interpreting ἡγήσατο has been partly got over by the substitution of a compound verb for the simple form. Yet it is not really got rid of, for ἐξηγέομαι can also mean "to take the lead," "to have the front place," and does not necessarily mean anything different from the πρωτεύειν of Paul.

Both writers, then, are working on the same theme, and working independently, but John is working more freely than Paul. The passage in Colossians resembles a list of the titles and offices of Christ, the Prologue in John is more like a poem, and in so far as it is poetic, is nearer to the Sapiential origins, even though in detail it may be more remote from them.

Consequently, if there is a Sophia-document missing, it underlies John rather than Paul, or if it underlies both of them, John is nearer to the form of the document.

As we have learnt a good deal by comparing the Colossian doctrine of the Logos with the Johannine, we make a further observation, and we notice that both writers have the doctrine of the Pleroma, which in later days, *i e* in Gnostic circles, acquired such prominence.

The Gospel has it in the form that "we have all received of the Pleroma of Jesus and grace for grace." The Epistle tells us that "according to the good pleasure of the Father all the Pleroma dwelt in the Son." After what we have already seen of the relation of the Gospel and Epistle *inter se*, it is not too much to say that they are working here from a common vocabulary. On the other hand, there does not seem to be any trace of the use of this word in the Sapiential Books upon which we have been working, and the word itself is so striking when used as expressing a communication of Divine Attributes, that we have a right to say that it has been found in some document intermediate between the Sapiential books and the New Testament. It may have been a hymn in praise of Sophia.

That it is Sophia who possesses the Pleroma may be seen in another way. The language of the Gospel is·

and we have all received of His Pleroma, grace piled on grace; for the law was given by Moses, Grace and Truth came by Jesus Christ.

The antithesis is recognised as being one between Law and Grace, the latter of which displaces the former. If, then, the writer is modifying a previous document and replacing Sophia by Jesus, we ought to have a sentence connecting Law and Truth with Sophia The missing sentence is found in Proverbs iii. 16·

> Out of her mouth goeth forth Righteousness,
> Law and Mercy she bears on her tongue.
> ἐκ τοῦ στόματος αὐτῆς ἐκπορεύεται δικαιοσύνη,
> νόμον δὲ καὶ ἔλεον ἐπὶ γλώσσης φορεῖ

The bridge between Proverbs (Law and Mercy) and the Gospel (Grace and Truth) will be found in Sap Sol. iii 9 (and iv. 15), Grace and Mercy to his elect.

> οἱ πεποιθότες ἐπ᾽ αὐτῷ συνήσουσιν ἀλήθειαν
> *   *   *   *   *
> ὅτι χάρις καὶ ἔλεος τοῖς ἐκλεκτοῖς αὐτοῦ (Sap Sol iii 9)

The suggestion to replace Law by Grace, so natural to the primitive Christian, had already been made in part by the Wisdom of Solomon. We can see the passages growing from one form to another before our eyes. But this will require that the Pleroma also should be a transfer from Sophia to Jesus. And I think that we may find the origin of the Pleroma: it was a Pleroma of Law. That was the way in which Wisdom was to find expression. In order to see this, we may take two related passages of Sirach, as follows:

> They that fear the Lord will seek out His good pleasure (εὐδοκίαν)
> And they that love Him will be filled with the Law (ἐμπλησθήσονται τοῦ νόμου).
> Sir. ii. 16.
> He that fears the Lord will accept chastening,
> And they that rise early will find His good pleasure (εὐδοκίαν);
> He that seeks Law will be filled with it (ἐμπλησθήσεται).
> Sir. xxxv. 14, 15.

The two passages are, as we have said, cognate: they imply a Pleroma of Law, and this is what pleases God; the Law is the Good Pleasure.

Now let us turn to Colossians and see how the Pleroma is introduced: we are told that "it was the Father's good pleasure that all the Pleroma should make its residence in the Son,"

> ἐν αὐτῷ εὐδόκησεν πᾶν τὸ πλήρωμα κατοικῆσαι,

where we have again the connexion between the εὐδοκία and the πλήρωμα.

The displacement of the Sophia that is interpreted as Law by the Sophia that is interpreted as Grace, may be illustrated from an actual equation made by the Jewish Fathers between Thorah

THE ORIGIN OF THE PROLOGUE TO ST JOHN 37

and Wisdom, as represented in the eighth chapter of Proverbs: thus in *Pirqe Aboth* (vi 10) we learn that the Holy One has five possessions in the world, of these, Thorah is one possession ... Thorah, whence? because it is written, *the Lord possessed me in the beginning of His way, before His works of old* (Prov. viii. 22). Here Sophia is clearly equated with Thorah

Other cases of the same equation will be found in Taylor (*Sayings of the Jewish Fathers*, ed. 2, p. 173), e g., Bereshith Rabbah begins with Proverbs viii 30, "Then was I by him as one brought up with him...and I was daily his delight as one brought up with him" Thorah is here identified with Wisdom, and is also made to say with reference to Proverbs *l.c*, "I was the instrument by which he created the world." See *Aboth* iii. 23. "Beloved are Israel that there was given to them the instrument with which the world was created"

We have assumed in the foregoing that the πλήρωμα is an experimental knowledge of the Law, in accordance with the statements of Sirach

> They that love Him *will be filled* with the Law (ii. 16),
> He that seeks Law *will be filled* with it (xxxv. 15).

In these passages we are almost bound to take the Law as an equivalent of *Wisdom*, just as in the *Sayings* of the Jewish Fathers, the Wisdom passage, Proverbs viii. 22, is made to apply directly to the *Thorah*, which is one of the Divine possessions, because "the Lord possessed me (Wisdom) in the beginning."

We thus see that there is a line of development of thought open, in which Christ will be announced not merely as Σοφία but also as Νόμος. It can be shown that this subordinate equation between Christ and Law was actually made, sometimes with the reservation that Christ is the *New* Law[1]. Thus Clement of

---

[1] B W Bacon in the *Story of St Paul*, p 317, makes the mistake of supposing Thorah to be anterior to Wisdom, whereas the evolution is evidently in the opposite direction He says

"Baruch (iii 29–37) simply substitutes for the word *Torah* in Deuteronomy (xxx 12–14) the philosophic term *Wisdom*, and Paul takes the next step and proceeds to identify this Wisdom in the heaven above and the abyss beneath with Christ"

It need hardly be pointed out that it was not Paul who identified Christ with Wisdom It was a part of the regular and official apostolic teaching, and had nothing to do with Deuteronomy in the first instance

Alexandria quotes the *Preaching of Peter* to prove that Christ is Νόμος and Λόγος:

> Νόμος καὶ Λόγος, αὐτὸς ὁ Σωτὴρ λέγεται, ὡς Πέτρος ἐν κηρύγματι
> *Eclogae in Script Proph* ii. 1004 (Potter).

The same thing occurs in a fragment of Hippolytus on *Luke* as follows:

> Luke ii 22 Ἱππολύτου ὅτε αὐτὸν ἀνήγαγον εἰς τὸ ἱερὸν παραστῆναι τῷ Κυρίῳ, τὰς καθαρσίους ἐπιτελοῦντες ἀναφοράς εἰ γὰρ τὰ καθάρσια δῶρα κατὰ τὸν νόμον ὑπὲρ αὐτοῦ προσφέρετο ταύτῃ καὶ ὑπὸ τὸν νόμον γέγονεν οὔτε δὲ ὁ Λόγος ὑπέκειτο τῷ νόμῳ, καθάπερ οἱ συκοφάνται δοξάζουσιν, αὐτὸς ὢν ὁ Νόμος
> (P.G 10. 701 A.)

There is another direction in which the idea of *Pleroma* might have been reached by the student of the Old Testament who was in search of Christ in its pages It is, in fact, said of the Holy Spirit that it fills the whole world:

> πνεῦμα Κυρίου πεπλήρωκεν τὴν οἰκουμένην, (Sap. Sol i 7)

and this passage is one of Gregory of Nyssa's proof-texts for the Holy Spirit It is, however, clear as we have shown by a variety of illustrations that the Holy Spirit came into the Christian Theology, through the bifurcation of the doctrine of the Divine Wisdom, which, on the one side, became the Logos, and on the other the Holy Ghost. It is Wisdom which is, in this passage, denoted by the Holy Spirit

It appears to be quite natural that the Law should turn up in the praises of Sophia, when Sophia is interpreted in a pre-Christian sense, and that it should be spoken of depreciatingly, when Sophia is interpreted in a Christian sense.

From the foregoing considerations it follows that there is an anti-Judaic element in the Fourth Gospel, from its very first page The Law is antagonised and the people to whom the Law came.

When we make that statement and follow Alford and Westcott in what is certainly the right explanation of "His own who did not receive Him," we are again treading on the heels of the first composers of books of Testimonies against the Jews, for a scrutiny of Cyprian's First Book of Testimonies shows conclusively the very same rejection of the Jews on the ground that they have rejected the Lord

THE ORIGIN OF THE PROLOGUE TO ST JOHN 39

Let us turn to the third chapter of the book in question. It is headed as follows.

That it was foretold that they (ι e the Jews) would neither recognise the Lord nor understand *nor receive Him.*

Then follow the proofs, and we readily anticipate the opening verses of Isaiah, with its appeal to a sinful nation, Israel that doth not know, my people that doth not understand. But a little lower down we come upon a reference to Proverbs i. 28 ff. · as follows:

Item apud Solomonem: Quaerent me mali et non inuenient. Oderunt enim *Sapientiam, sermonem* autem *Domini non receperunt.*

Here we have the Logos and Sophia side by side in the same verse, and the statement that the Wisdom has been hated and the Word not received   The parallel with John i. 11 is obvious. That verse is of the nature of an anti-Judaic Testimony. It is an adaptation of the LXX of Proverbs i 29

ἐμίσησαν γὰρ σοφίαν, τὸν δὲ λόγον τοῦ Κυρίου οὐ προσείλαντο

The transition from σοφία to λόγος is natural and easy, and a primitive statement that Wisdom came to the Jews and the Jews did not receive her, would readily be re-written in terms of the Logos, who

Came to His own, and His own did not receive Him

The two statements are in part equivalent; and Alford's interpretation was right as far as it went.

In this connexion belongs a curious chapter in the Book of Enoch, which Dr Charles had actually suggested to be parallel with the Prologue of John

The forty-second chapter of Enoch opens as follows

Wisdom found no place where she might dwell,
Then a dwelling place was assigned her in the heavens
Wisdom came to make her dwelling among the children of men,
    And found no dwelling place,
Then Wisdom returned to her place,
    And took her seat among the angels.

The parallels with the Logos who dwelt among us, and who had not been received by His own, are striking. And we are confirmed in our belief that the Prologue to the Gospel can be turned back from a Logos-Hymn to a Sophia-Hymn.

One more illustration may be given of the derivation of the language of the Prologue from the Sapiential sources which preceded it

The Gospel, after reciting the unresponsiveness of the Jewish people generally to the Logos who had come among them, goes on to explain that there were some who did receive the Logos, and that, in consequence of this reception, they became *children of God*, and experienced a spiritual birth, "to as many as received Him, to them gave He power to become the children of God, owing their birth not to carnal generation nor human impulse, but to the Divine Will[1]." It may be asked whether this striking passage has any counterpart in the Sophia literature upon which we have been drawing

The answer is that to this beautiful description of the appearance of the Life of the Spirit as given in the Gospel, there is a parallel, shorter indeed, but almost as beautiful, in the seventh chapter of the Wisdom of Solomon, from which we have already taken so many illustrations. "In all ages Wisdom entering into holy souls, makes them *Friends of God* and prophets"

It is this work of Sophia in the making of "Friends of God" ($\phi i\lambda ous\ \Theta \epsilon o\hat{u}$) that has prompted the "Children of God" ($\tau \epsilon \kappa \nu a\ \Theta \epsilon o\hat{u}$) who result from the reception of the Logos[2]

In explaining $\dot{\epsilon}\xi\eta\gamma\eta\sigma ato$ of John i. 18 as being the equivalent of $\dot{\eta}\gamma\eta\sigma\acute{a}\mu\eta\nu$ in Sirach xxiv 6, we have found the reason for the little inserted testimony of John the Baptist in John i. 15, which is also occupied with the doctrine of the priority and primacy of Jesus. It may, however, be urged that in thus changing the interpretation of $\dot{\epsilon}\xi\eta\gamma\eta\sigma ato$, we have broken sequence with the statement that precedes it as to the "invisibility of God," whom it is the business of the Unique-Born Logos to *expound* to men

The sentence as to the invisibility of God is another Sapiential loan: it is parallel to Colossians i. 15

$$\ddot{o}s\ \dot{\epsilon}\sigma\tau\iota\nu\ \epsilon i\kappa\grave{\omega}\nu\ \tau o\hat{v}\ \theta\epsilon o\hat{v}\ \tau o\hat{v}\ \dot{a}o\rho\acute{a}\tau ov,$$

where it is followed by

$$\pi\rho\omega\tau\acute{o}\tau o\kappa os\ \pi\acute{a}\sigma\eta s\ \kappa\tau\acute{\iota}\sigma\epsilon\omega s$$

just as the passage in John is followed by the reference to the *Monogenēs*: both sequences are Sapiential, and are suggestive of a common document and a common sequence of thought. In such a document $\dot{\eta}\gamma\eta\sigma\acute{a}\mu\eta\nu$ must be interpreted in the sense that

---

[1] If we follow the very early reading ὅς ἐγεννήθη the latter part of the sentence relates to the Logos, and goes back to ὁ κύριος γεννᾷ με of Proverbs viii 25

[2] Hence, perhaps, the masculine oἵ in John i 13

Sophia had the first rank, after God, in the order of being. Note carefully that neither in Sirach nor in John is there any object attached to ἡγέομαι. it is therefore, to be taken intransitively. The case of ἐκδιηγήσομαι in Sirach xlii. 15, xliv 31 is, therefore, not an objection to the intransitive interpretation, for here the object is expressed

Was there anything in the underlying document that corresponded to the statement that "the Word became flesh"? Will the critical reagent bring it up?

Suppose we turn to Methodius, the *Banquet of the Ten Virgins* (III. 4, P. G. IX 18 65), we shall find a very curious passage, whose obscurity has baffled both translators and interpreters The writer has been explaining the difficulties which arise from the Pauline language when the Apostle compares Christ and the Church mystically with Adam and Eve in the Book of Genesis How could the comparison have been made between the pure and the impure? we might as well compare odd and even. No wonder that persons have taken exception to the comparison between the First Adam and the Second Methodius explains that it was the Wisdom of God that was joined to the First Adam, and became incarnate. and this Wisdom was Christ His language is very peculiar, and needs closer examination

It was appropriate, says Methodius, that Wisdom (the Firstborn, the First Offshoot, the Only-Born of God) should be united with the First and First-Born Man (Adam) by an incarnation We notice the array of Sapiential terms with which we have become familiar

The result of this incarnation was Christ, "a man filled with the pure and perfect Godhead, and God received into man." In other words, *Christ is the Incarnate Wisdom of God* Thus there lies behind the phrase

$$\text{ὁ λόγος σὰρξ ἐγένετο,}$$

the expression

$$\text{ἡ σοφία σὰρξ ἐγένετο}$$

If Christ is Firstborn, and Only-born, He has derived these appellations from Sophia.

Methodius continues the explanation· "it was most suitable that the oldest of the aeons and the first of the Archangels (viz. Sophia), when about to hold communion with men, should dwell in the oldest and the first of men, even in Adam." The passage suggests for Sophia a description almost identical with the Johannine language, that "the Word became Flesh", for "the Word" restore "Wisdom"

It is interesting to note further that Methodius has elsewhere identified Christ with the Wisdom of God, by a combination of the language of Proverbs with that of St John's Gospel In his discourse on the Resurrection, he tells us that "Wisdom, the Firstborn of God, the parent and artificer of all things, brings forth everything into the world ..whom the ancients called Nature and Providence, because she, with constant provision and care, gives to all things birth and growth For, *says the Wisdom of God,* 'my Father worketh still, and I work' (John v. 17)." We note the identification of Jesus with the Wisdom of God, and compare the way in which the passage from John is introduced with the similar feature which we observed in the Gospel of Luke (xi. 49)

An even more remarkable equation between Christ and the Wisdom of God will be found in the fragments of Methodius on *Created Things,* which are preserved for us in the *Bibliotheca* of Photius Here the equivalence of the opening verses of the Prologue with the eighth chapter of Proverbs is insisted upon:

> Methodius says, of the words "In the Beginning God created the Heavens and the earth," that one will not err who says that the Beginning is Wisdom For Wisdom is said by one of the Divine Band to speak in this manner concerning herself "The Lord created me the Beginning of His ways for His works; from eternity He laid my foundation" It was fitting and more seemly that all things which came into existence should be more recent than Wisdom, since they existed through her. Now, consider whether this saying "In the beginning was the Word, and the Word was with God and the Word was God,"—whether these statements be not in agreement with those
>
> (Photius, *Bibliotheca,* Cod. 235)

The doctrine of Methodius appears to have been that Sophia became incarnate in the First Adam and also in the Second In the eighth chapter of the *Banquet* he sums up the results of his mystical investigations as follows.

> It has been already established by no contemptible arguments from Scripture, that the first man may probably be referred to Christ Himself, and is no longer a type and representation and image of the Only-Begotten, but has actually become Wisdom and Word

THE ORIGIN OF THE PROLOGUE TO ST JOHN 43

There is still a good deal of obscurity in the statements of Methodius, but it is quite clear that the Incarnation of which he speaks is the Incarnation of Wisdom. Whether it is Christ or Adam or both that are the subject of the Incarnation is not quite clear.

Now let us try to restore the Prologue to something like its intermediate form It should run as follows:

Prov. viii. 22 ff : The Beginning was Wisdom,
                Wisdom was with God,
Sap. Sol. ix. 4: Wisdom was the assessor of God.
                All things were made by her;
                Apart from her nothing that was made came to be.
Sap. Sol vi. 26: With her was Light, and the Light was the Life of men.
                That Light shone in the Darkness,
Sap. Sol vi 29: And the Darkness did not overmaster it
                For no evil overmasters Wisdom.
                Wisdom was in the World,
                In the World which she had made,
Prov. 1 28. The world did not recognise her.
Sir. xxxiv 13 ff. ·⎫
Enoch xli. 1 ff : ⎬ She came to the Jews, and the Jews did not receive her.
Sap Sol. vii 27· Those that did receive her became Friends of God and
                prophets.
Sir. xxxiv. 6: ⎱ She tabernacled with us, and we saw her splendour, the
Sap. Sol vii 25: ⎰   splendour of the Father's Only Child,
Sap Sol. iii 9   Full of Grace and Truth
Ode Sol. 33   (She declared the Grace of God among us).
Sir xxxv. 15. From her pleroma we have received Grace instead of Law,
                For Law came by Moses,
Sap Sol iii. 19·   Grace and Mercy came by Sophia;
Sap. Sol. ix. 26 She is the Image of the Invisible God,
Sap Sol vi 22·⎱ She is the only Child of God, in the bosom of the Father,
Sir xxxiv 6. ⎰   and has the primacy

CHRIST AS THE HAND OF GOD

When we study the surviving texts of that very early Christian book, known as the *Testimonies against the Jews*, we find that one of the things which has to be established against the Jews is that *Christ is the Hand of God*; one does not at first see the reason for this statement nor for the emphasis laid upon it· yet it is clear that it occupies an early and an important position amongst the theses which the primitive Christian nailed on the doors of the Synagogue. In the second book of Cyprian's *Testimonies*, for example (that section which contains the Christology,—it is important to remember that primitive Christian propaganda *is* primitive Christology), we find that the fourth place in the list of propositions to be discussed and defended is the statement that

The same Christ is the hand and the arm of God.

The preceding theses are concerned with the proof that Christ is the Wisdom of God, and the Word of God. Why should these high-level statements in theology drop down to such an unexpected piece of exegetical poverty as that Christ is the Hand of God?

The first thing that suggests itself is that the author of the theses is following the way of escape, which Jewish theologians of a progressive type had found, out of the temptations to anthropomorphism in the O.T. We may imagine the situation as it would occur to an Alexandrian of the school of Philo, or to a Palestinian thinker, who has to explain away the speech of God, and the walk of God, and the form of God, and the eyes, hands, organs and dimensions of God. He has to be rid of all these without getting rid at the same time of God and of the activity of God. This can only be done by the introduction of a subordinate being, who shall bear the name of God, and possess in a sufficient degree His attributes, or by the philosophical hypostasis and personification of the attributes themselves, either simply or in combination; that is, an angelic or archangelic person, or a supra-sensual idea. Then, if the Jewish world has already, in the person of its leading thinkers, attained to such a theological re-construction as may secure them, when they revile the Olympians, from a counter-revilement, it will be easy for the Christian polemist to explain to the Jews that they have in reality discovered the Christ; have, in fact, in running away from the dread spectre of a pursuing anthropomorphism, run into his very arms, the arms of God; the everlasting ones of that species of representation being the arms of Christ!

Such a method of expounding the nature of the first Christian propaganda cannot be altogether wide of the mark: but it is always as well, in reconstructing a lost, or studying a nascent theology, to let the documents talk first, and say all that they have to say on the subject, before we ascend the rostrum ourselves.

CHRIST AS THE HAND OF GOD

We need to consider, for example, the continuity of the theses discussed, and the light thrown on them by contemporary or subsequent literature Why does the doctrine of the Hand follow so closely on the doctrine of the Wisdom and the doctrine of the Word? The answer is a curious one: the fourth thesis of the second book of *Testimonies against the Jews* is based upon an earlier form in which it was said,

That the same Wisdom is the Hand of God.

We establish this thesis, which takes us to a somewhat different point of view (but not altogether diverse), in the following way. In the *Clementine Homilies* (which contain so much early controversial matter by way of survival), we have in the sixteenth Homily a dispute between Peter and Simon Magus over the Divine Unity. Simon challenges the consistency of the doctrine of the Unity with the language of Genesis (1 26) "Let us make man," etc , and Peter replies as follows.

He who said to His Wisdom, Let us make, is one. And His Wisdom is that with which He always joyed as though it were His own spirit: for She is united as Soul to God. *and is stretched out by Him as a Hand for the creation of the world.*

καὶ ὁ Πέτρος ἀπεκρίνατο εἷς ἐστὶν ὁ τῇ αὐτοῦ Σοφίᾳ εἰπών· ποιήσωμεν ἄνθρωπον ἡ δὲ Σοφία, ᾗ ὥσπερ ἰδίῳ πνεύματι αὐτὸς ἀεὶ συνέχαιρεν (Prov viii 30) ἥνωται γὰρ ὡς ψυχὴ τῷ Θεῷ ἐκτείνεται δὲ ὑπ' αὐτοῦ, ὡς χείρ, δημιουργοῦσα τὸν κόσμον   Clem Hom xvi 12.

If Wisdom is the Hand of God, and the Creative Instrument, we see why the statement to that effect occupies the position that it does in the Testimony Book The whole of the passage quoted is of interest, and is redolent of antiquity. The great stumbling-block for monotheists in the first chapter of Genesis, is explained by a duality in God, rather than a Trinity. Simon says, "Let us make" implies two or more. *There are, says he, evidently two who created.* Peter accepts it and identifies the second Creator with the Sophia of the eighth chapter of Proverbs There is the Begotten God and the Unbegotten; the latter makes the World by the former. ·

When we turn to examine the actual Testimonies quoted in Cyprian we have first a passage from Is lix. 1, "Is the Lord's hand shortened, etc.," and it is clear from the context that this passage is quoted rather to show the sinfulness of the Jews than the nature of the Divine Hand. "Your iniquities have separated between you and God," etc.

Then follows a reference to the "arm of the Lord," etc in Is lviii. 1, evidently brought in for the sake of the "arm" and contributing nothing immediate to its explanation

After that we come to Is. lxvi. 1 ff., which leads up to the enquiry

> Hath not my hand made all these things?

viz : Heaven and Earth.

This is the creative Hand again. Lower down we have a long passage from Is. xli. 15 ff , ending up with

> The Hand of the Lord hath made all these things:

here again we are concerned with creative and redemptive acts attributed to the Hand of God; and for this Divine Hand we have given the primary explanation; it is the Divine Wisdom.

It will be interesting to see how this interpretation that the Hand of God is His Wisdom, by which He instrumentally made the world, can be reconciled with correct theology. The interpretation is clearly ancient, and it labours under a difficulty, in that it represents God as a Duality, and not as a Trinity In the dispute between Peter and Simon Magus in the Clementine story, this is conceded on both sides. It is, however, clear that it will have to be modified, or there will be theological friction. The way of escape is to say that *God has two hands* or creative instruments, viz : (i) His Wisdom, (ii) His Word, or, comprehending them under a single formula, His Word and His Wisdom.

If we want to see the formulae in process of evolution, we may turn to the pages of Irenaeus. We are told (see Iren p. 218 Mass) that Adam was made of Virgin earth, and was "fashioned by the *Hand of God, i e. by the Word of God*," according to the saying of John that all things were made by Him Here the Word has been substituted for the Wisdom in the definition of the Hand

Somewhat later (p. 228), Irenaeus repeats the statement that man was formed in the similitude of God, and was fashioned *by His hands*, viz , *by the Son and the Spirit*, those to whom He was speaking when He said, Let us make man. Here the Son has replaced the Logos, and the Spirit stands for Sophia. Both of the Creative Hands are in operation. Further on (p. 253), we come to the statement that the angels could not be responsible for the creation of man, since *God had His own Hands*. "He had *always by Him the Word and the Wisdom, the Son and the Spirit through whom and in whom of His own free will He made all things, and whom He addresses when He says, Let us make man in our own image and likeness"*

Here we find the Son and Spirit side by side with the Word and Wisdom with whom they have been equated[1]. The same interpretation of "Let us make" is found elsewhere in the Fathers; sometimes it is explained of the co-operation of the Logos, and sometimes of Logos and Sophia For example, in Theophilus *ad Autolycum* (c 18), the two Hands of God are implied, and they are the Word and the Wisdom:

> He considers the creation of man alone worthy His own hands. Nay, further, as if needing assistance, we find God saying, "Let us make man in our image and likeness" but He said "Let us make" *to none other than His own Logos and Sophia*

The same tradition re-appears in Procopius of Gaza[2], "the Hands of God are the Son and the Holy Spirit," where we have clearly an evolution from the earlier statement as to Logos and Sophia.

In Clement of Alexandria the doctrine of one hand is commonly involved, for he interprets ποιήσωμεν in Gen i 26 as addressed to the Logos.

The transition from "one hand" to "two hands" in the description of the instruments by which Creation was effected, may be seen very clearly in Tertullian's *Treatise against Hermogenes*: after contesting the belief of Hermogenes as to the eternity of matter on philosophical grounds, he turns to the evidence of the Scriptures and the teaching of the prophets·

> They did not mention matter but said that *Wisdom* was *first* set up, the beginning of His ways for His works (Prov viii. 22); then that *the Word* was produced through whom all things were made, and without whom nothing was made (John i 3) He (the Word) is the *Lord's right hand, indeed His two hands*, by which He worked and fashioned. For, says He, the Heavens are the works *of thine hands* (Ps. cii 25) wherewith He hath meted out the Heaven, *and the earth with a span* (Is xl 12, xlviii 13) Adv Hermogenem, c 45.

[1] The Son and the Spirit as the Hands of God will be found again in Irenaeus (p 327) as follows

"Et propter hoc in omni tempore plasmatus initio homo per manus Dei, id est, Filii et Spiritus. fit secundum imaginem et similitudinem Dei"

Here again the reference to the creation of man shows that the first stage of the doctrine which Irenaeus presents was a reflection upon the words "Let us make man," according to which it was explained that God spoke to His Wisdom, which was His Hand, i e to the Word and the Wisdom which were His hands, i e to the Son and the Spirit The growth of the successive statements is clearly made out

[2] P. G 87 134 A

The reasoning borders on the Rabbinical method, but it is not to be condemned on that account as non-primitive; the course of the argument clearly shows the stages by which Wisdom was replaced by the Word, and the Hand of God (His Wisdom or His Word) was replaced by His two Hands, which were His Wisdom and His Word.

We shall find that the same theology prevails in the writings of Athanasius and Augustine, both of whom identify Christ with the Wisdom of God by whom the worlds were made, and both of whom apply the title "Hand of God" to Christ.

For instance, Athanasius tells us[1] that we may learn from the Scriptures themselves that Christ is the Word of God and the Wisdom, and the Image, *and the Hand* and the Power." He quotes the appropriate Scriptures, and when he comes to the first three verses of John, tells us that John composed his Gospel, because he knew that the Word is the Wisdom and *the Hand* of God." And Augustine says expressly that "The Hand of the Father is the Son[2]"

These references may easily be multiplied they show us clearly that the doctrine that Christ is the Word of God does not arise, in the first instance, from a sentiment adverse to anthropomorphic representations of God; for, as we have abundantly made clear, we start from the position that Christ is the Wisdom of God, an earlier position than the hypostatising of a supposed Memra, and indeed, the Memra in the sense of the Targums does not appear in our investigations. Neither do we start from Creation, as Creation is described in the first chapter of Genesis. Our point of departure is the Book of Proverbs, especially the eighth chapter, with an occasional divergence into the Psalter, Genesis comes later in the argument, when we explain "Let us make man," Wisdom is introduced, already identified with the Creative Instrument from Proverbs This Wisdom is either the Divine Conjugate or the Divine Offspring; it is not quite clear which If the former, the Logos is her Son; if the latter, the Logos is her brother. The former position leads on to the curious Word of Christ in the *Gospel of the Hebrews*, "My Mother the Holy Ghost," the latter to the twinship of Jesus and the Holy Spirit, as we find it in the *Pistis Sophia* When the Logos becomes also

---

[1] *De Secretis Nicaenae Synodi*, § 17 ff
[2] *In Joann* xlviii. 7   *Enarr in Ps* cxviii   Serm 23, 5 and 143, 14

an Assessor Dei, we have the Christian Trinity: but behind this there is the earlier stratum of a Christian Duality (the Holy Spirit being not yet come, in a theological sense, because the Divine Wisdom has not been divided into Logos and Pneuma).

We now begin to see that the controversy between Arius and Athanasius is not a mere struggle of an orthodox Church with an aggressive and cancerous heresy: the heretic is the orthodox conservative, and the supposed orthodox champion is the real progressive The conflict is one between two imperfectly harmonised strata of belief. Arius and Athanasius do not stand at opposite poles: they are really next-door neighbours. This appears, *inter alia*, from the fact that they practically use the same traditional Scripture proofs; we have shown elsewhere how painfully faithful Athanasius is to the body of conventional Christian Testimonies. It is not, however, that Arius is at heart a Jew, and must be struck down with the weapons proper to anti-Judaic struggle. Arius is as much anti-Judaic as Athanasius; only his collection of Testimonies has not been completed as to the text, and still less as to the interpretation Both of the great protagonists begin by saying the same words,

The Lord created me the Beginning,

both of them explain that Christ is here speaking in the person of Wisdom Neither of them doubts that ἔκτισέν με (the Lord created me) is applicable to Christ, though it was a false rendering of the Septuagint: they differ when they come to harmonise the Divine Creation with the other statement that Wisdom was older than the worlds and was the first-born of God. Athanasius explains that the Christ is a creature, but *not as one of the creatures*, he saves his proof-text at the expense of its natural meaning: Arius explains away the eternity of the Divine Wisdom, by saying that Wisdom is eternal relatively to the Creation, but not eternal relatively to God[1].

Now if we bear in mind the facts which we have established, that the Nicene conflict is concerned with two different strata of the traditional proof-texts for primitive Church doctrine, we shall find it very much easier to see our way through the smoke of the conflict into the real meaning of the battle. That Athanasius

---

[1] Hence I was wrong in saying in *Testimonia* that it was not inept for Athanasius to have felled Arius to the ground with a missile borrowed from *Testimonies against the Jews*. Both of the combatants were anti-Judaic.

himself is in possession of the whole story, and the evolution of the doctrine of the Trinity, will be clear now to the readers of his *Orations against the Arians,* which run over with the matters which the Church had discussed in the centuries that preceded him In order to illustrate this point we take a single passage from Athanasius and hold it up in the light of the discoveries which we have made as to the origin and growth of the Christian tradition.

In his second *Oration against the Arians* Athanasius says as follows: "All things that were made, were made by the Hand, and the Wisdom of God, for God Himself says:

> My Hand hath made all these things (Is lxvi. 2 ff.)

and David sings:

> Thou Lord in the beginning hast laid the foundations of the earth and the Heavens are the work of Thy hands (Ps ci. 26)

And again in the 142nd Psalm:

> I remembered the days of old,
> I meditated on all thy works;
> On the works of thy hands did I meditate

So then the things made were wrought by the Hand of God, for it is written that

> All things were made by the Word
> And without Him was nothing made (John i. 3)

And again, there is

> One Lord Jesus, by whom all things are made (1 Cor. viii. 6),

and

> In Him all things exist (Col i. 17).

So it must be obvious that the Son cannot be a work of God, but is Himself *the Hand of God and the Wisdom.*

The martyrs of Babylon understood this, Ananias, Azarias and Misael, and they confute the impiety of the Arians, for they say

> O all ye works of the Lord, bless ye the Lord.

They did not say 'Bless the Lord, Logos, and praise Him, Sophia'; in order to show that all the rest that praise are God's works, but the Logos is not the work of God nor of the company that praise, but is with the Father the object of praise and worship, and is reckoned Divine ($\theta\epsilon o\lambda o\gamma o\acute{u}\mu\epsilon\nu o\varsigma$), *being the Word and His Wisdom, and the Artificer of His works.* The same thing is expressed by the Spirit in the Psalms with an excellent distinction between the Word and the Works,

> *The Word of* the Lord is right,
> And *all His works* are in faith.

Just as it says elsewhere,

> O Lord, how great are *Thy works*
> Thou hast made them all *in Wisdom*."

Here we have gathered together in a single statement as to the origin of the Creation the doctrine that Christ is (*a*) the Wisdom of God; (*b*) the Word of God, (*c*) the Hand of God, and that the two Hands of God are, in fact, His Word and His Wisdom.

The difference between Arius and Athanasius is a question whether the Hand of God is co-eternal with God Himself; did God make the Hand by which He made the world?

As we have several times indicated, the Christian statements which we find in the Fourth Gospel are not derived immediately from Philo and his speculative Logos. The two evolutions of doctrine are very nearly independent of one another. It is interesting to see that Philo has the same problem before him, of the relation of the hypostatised Wisdom to God, and to observe how differently the problem of the Persons is worked out. In one passage Philo makes Wisdom the Divine conjugate, and the Divine Son is the Cosmos. Thus we have the following Trinity:

God = Sophia
|
The only-begotten Son, who is the world

That Sophia is really here the Mother will appear from a study of the passage which we transcribe·

"We shall affirm that the Mother of the created thing is *Understanding*, with whom God had intercourse (not in a mundane sense) and begat creation (ἔσπειρε γένεσιν). She it was who received the Divine seed, and by a perfect child-bearing (τελεσφόροις ὠδῖσι) brought forth the Only Son, the Beloved, the Perceptible One (αἰσθητόν), the World."

And by one of the Choir of Heavenly Singers Wisdom is introduced as speaking of herself on this wise:

"The Lord *possessed* me the foremost (πρωτίστην) of his works, and before eternity he founded me. For of necessity all those things which came into being are younger than the One who is the Mother and the nurse of the Universe (τῶν ὅλων)." Philo, *De Ebrietate* i. 362.

Here we see Philo wrestling with a similar problem to that of the early Christian thinkers; he agrees with them in reference to the relation of Wisdom to the Divine Nature, and differs from them altogether with reference to the Divine Son · and, as has often been pointed out by recent theologians, the differences between Philo and St John (or St Paul) are more conspicuous than the agreements.

ON THE ASCRIPTION OF SAPIENTIAL TITLES TO CHRIST

We have shown in what precedes that the recognition of Christ as the Wisdom of God led to the ascription to Him of all those titles and qualities attached to Wisdom in the Sapiential books, and that the primitive Christology was largely made up out of such ascriptions. Some of these titles were easily recognised from their employment in the Epistle to the Colossians or the Epistle to the Hebrews: but there were others that were not so clearly identified. Take for example, the statement that "Wisdom is the unsullied mirror of the Divine activity"; it was not quite easy to establish the equation between Christ and the Mirror of God in the New Testament; but at this point the *Odes of Solomon* came to our aid and we found the 13th Ode opening with the statement

> Behold! the Lord is our mirror!

In commenting upon this I drew attention to the occurrence of the identification that we are trying to establish in the pseudo-Cyprianic tract *De montibus Sina et Sion*. I transcribe portions of the comment referred to.

> We may also in this connexion refer to a remarkable passage, which is found in a tract falsely ascribed to Cyprian, and known as *De montibus Sina et Sion* We are reminded in this passage first that Christ is the Unspotted Mirror of the Father, as is said of Wisdom in the book called the Wisdom of Solomon (Sap. Sol. vii. 26).

Hence the Father and the Son see one another by reflexion. The writer then continues as follows:

> And even we who believe in Him see Christ in us as in a mirror, as He Himself instructs and advises us in the Epistle of His disciple John to the

people: "See me in yourselves, in the same way as any one of you sees himself in water or in a mirror", and so He confirmed the saying of Solomon about Himself, that "He is the unspotted mirror of the Father."

When I wrote this comment I had hardly noticed the underlying identification of Christ with Sophia, and certainly did not recognise that the "mirror" was a part of the identification. Now that the Sophia Christology has come to light, we can understand the language of the Ode and of the author of *De montibus* a great deal better[1]. So much concerning Christ as the Spotless Mirror. Now let us try a more difficult case. The same chapter of the Wisdom of Solomon describes Wisdom as a breath (*or* vapour) of the power of God: ἀτμὶς τῆς τοῦ θεοῦ δυνάμεως. The question arises naturally enough whether this term ἀτμίς has been taken up into Christology, and applied to Christ It hardly seems likely at the first glance: if anything has been transferred from this expression it would be the simple "Power of God" and not anything so doubtful of meaning as "Vapour of the Power of God." Christ the *Power of God* and the Wisdom of God may very well have been derived from this, but where shall we find Christ described as ἀτμίς?

We do find it.

If we turn to a fragment of Theognostus of Alexandria (one of the heads of the famous catechetical school) preserved for us in the epistle of Athanasius *De Decretis Nicenae Synodi*[2] we shall find Theognostus speaking of the nature of the Son of God as follows:

> He was born of the substance of the Father, as the ἀπαύγασμα from the light, *and as the* ἀτμίς from the water; the ἀτμίς is not the water; nor is the ἀπαύγασμα the Sun itself, though not of another nature to it. Christ is an ἀπόρροια from the substance of the Father.

So here is ἀτμίς coupled with two other Sapiential terms from the same connexion:

> ἀτμὶς γάρ ἐστιν τῆς τοῦ θεοῦ δυνάμεως,
> καὶ ἀπόρροια τῆς τοῦ παντοκράτορος δόξης εἰλικρινής·
> ἀπαύγασμα γάρ ἐστιν φωτὸς ἀιδίου (Sap Sol. vii. 25, 26).

There can be no doubt that Theognostus is interpreting the seventh chapter of Wisdom and that he equates ἀτμίς with Christ, as well as ἀπαύγασμα and ἀπόρροια.

---

[1] Incidentally we may note that Ephrem had no right to alter the 13th Ode in the interests of Baptism and read it as "The water is our mirror."
[2] Routh, *Rell* iii, 411.

The same interpretation occurs in Dionysius of Alexandria

φωτὸς μὲν οὖν ὄντος τοῦ Θεοῦ, ὁ Χριστός ἐστιν ἀπαύγασμα, πνεύματος δὲ ὄντος (πνεῦμα γὰρ, φησὶν, ὁ Θεός), ἀναλόγως πάλιν ὁ Χριστὸς ἀτμὶς λέγεται· Ἀτμὶς γὰρ, φησὶν, ἐστὶ τῆς τοῦ Θεοῦ δυνάμεως
(Athan *Ep de sent. Dionys.* xv.: in Routh, *Rell.* iii 391)

It is interesting in view of the proved use of Sapiential language by the author of the Odes of Solomon to which we adverted above, to note that Gressmann thinks he has found the ἀτμίς also in the Odes. The immediately preceding Ode, the twelfth, is concerned with the powers and qualities of Christ as the Logos, and some of its expressions are almost certainly Sapiential. We have in v. 5 the following sequence:

For the swiftness of the Word is inexpressible;
And like its expression (!) is its swiftness and its sharpness.

The first line of this is a versification of Sap Sol vii 24 ("Wisdom is more mobile than any motion"); and in the next line Gressmann suggests that we read ܟܘܚ for ܟܘܐܚ, 'and like an ἀτμίς is its swiftness,' etc., by a very slight change in the Syriac; this emendation makes parallelism with Sap. Sol vii 25.

No doubt the proposed emendation will be estimated in the forthcoming facsimile edition of the Odes. At present we merely draw attention to it There seems no doubt that Ode xii of the Solomonic collection is working over the seventh chapter of Wisdom and kindred matters. The "sharpness" of the Word, to which allusion is made above, is taken from Sap. Sol. vii. 22, where the Spirit of Wisdom is described as

σαφές, ἀπήμαντον, φιλάγαθον, <u>ὀξύ</u>

The foregoing enquiry brings out clearly that ἀπαύγασμα and ἀτμίς are Christological terms, and attaches to them the ἀπόρροια. It is probable that this term also, which occupies such an important position in the *Odes of Solomon*, is originally Sapiential in origin, and is a term for the Sophia-Christ.

We noted in the earlier pages of this work that there was one passage in Hebrews which was usually explained by Philonean parallels, the passage which speaks of the Word as "quick and powerful and sharper than a sword with two edges, and penetrating to the division of soul and spirit" (Heb. iv. 12). It has been suggested to me[1] that we should abandon the references to Philo,

---
[1] By my friend, C. A Phillips.

OF SAPIENTIAL TITLES TO CHRIST

and derive the language directly from the Book of Wisdom. The comparison would have to be made between

Heb	Sap Sol.
ἐνεργής	ἐνεργητικόν (?)
τομώτερος	ὀξύ
διικνούμενος κτέ	διήκει καὶ χωρεῖ κτέ

The matter certainly deserves a careful consideration, in view of the obvious loans from Wisdom in the first chapter of Hebrews Our conclusion that all these Sapiential terms, the ἀπαύγασμα, the ἀπόρροια, the ἀτμίς, the εἰκών and the rest have been transferred to Christ in the earliest period of the crystallisation of Christian Theology may be confirmed by the following passage from Origen *De Principiis*. we shall find that Origen tries to show that the Sapiential titles were to be recognised indeed as titles of Christ, but that the derivation was in the opposite-order; they were hers (Wisdom's) because they were His.

Ait apostolus Paulus unigenitum filium imaginem esse Dei invisibilis, et primogenitum eum esse totius creaturae· ad Hebraeos vero scribens dicit de eo, quia sit splendor gloriae et figura expressa substantiae eius Invenimus nihilominus etiam in Sapientia quae dicitur Salomonis, descriptionem de Dei sapientia hoc modo scriptam · vapor est enim, inquit, virtutis Dei, et ἀπόρροια gloriae omnipotentis purissima: ideo ergo in eam nihil commaculatum incidere potest. Splendor enim est lucis aeternae et speculum immaculatum operationis Dei, et imago bonitatis ejus. Sapientiam vero dicimus, sicut superius diximus, subsistentiam habentem non alibi nisi in eo qui est initium omnium; ex quo et nata est quaeque sapientia, quia ipse est qui solus natura filius, idcirco et unigenitus dicitur (*De Principiis* 1. 2. 5).

So runs the passage in Ruffinus' translation, who would have done better in translating Μονογενής in the last sentence, to render it *unigenita*, for it is clearly a title of Wisdom The translator was bewitched by the author to regard Christ as the original *Only-Begotten*. The argument is resumed as follows: after quoting Sap. vii. 25 with its statement that Wisdom is the ἀτμίς of the Divine Power, etc :

Quae ergo hic de Deo definit, ex singulis quibusque certo quaedam inesse Sapientiae Dei designat: virtutem namque Dei nominat, et gloriam et lucem aeternam, et inoperationem et bonitatem Ait autem Sapientiam vaporem esse non gloriae omnipotentis, neque aeternae lucis, nec inspirationis patris, nec bonitatis eius. neque enim conveniens erat alicui horum adscribi vaporem; sed eum omni proprietate ait virtutis Dei vaporem esse Sapientiam. .

Secundum Apostolum vero dicentem, quia Christus Dei virtus est (1 Cor. 1 24), jam non solum vapor virtutis Dei, sed virtus ex virtute dicenda (*Ibid.* 1. 2, 9).

This is a very interesting passage; it shows that when the Sapiential term ἀτμίς was applied to Christ, it was taken as we suggested above, in the sense of ἀτμὶς δυνάμεως. It is also evident that Origen is still arguing that Christ is Sophia because Sophia is Christ; He is derived from her because she is derived from Him: for that reason if Wisdom is Power, she might more correctly be spoken of as "Power of Power." If Origen had taken the argument a little further, he might have reduced it even more clearly *ad absurdum*: for since Sophia is the ἀρχή since "the Lord created me the ἀρχή," etc., and Christ is also the ἀρχή of the Creation of God, according to the Apostle, it follows that Wisdom is the Beginning because Christ is the Beginning, and might, therefore, be described as ἀρχὴ ἐξ ἀρχῆς, a Beginning derived from a Beginning!

We have shown again in the course of the discussion that ἀτμίς is a true term for Christ, though it is veiled in the Pauline Epistles by the use of the term "Power of God"; and that ἀτμίς, ἀπόρροια and the rest are all terms that are involved in the primitive theology of the Church

Here is a further piece of evidence that Jesus was familiarly known as the *Wisdom of God* in certain early Christian circles.

We have referred from time to time in this investigation to the *Dialogues between Christians and Jews*, of which the earliest example is the *Dialogue between Jason and Papiscus* by Ariston of Pella, which is lost, though no doubt it survives in a number of more or less modified descendants: amongst these one of the most interesting is the *Dialogue between Athanasius and Zacchaeus* published some years since by Mr F C Conybeare. In this *Dialogue* the points of the *Testimony Book* turn up to such an extent, that the *Dialogue* may be treated as a literary recast of the other anti-Judaic document In the course of the argument Zacchaeus challenges the statement of Athanasius that Christ is spoken of in the prophets as the Λίθος. "Do you mean to say," he interjects," that *the Wisdom of God* is a Stone?' Athanasius has to explain the sense in which these typical terms are used and to give him illustrations.

When Athanasius demonstrates from the Old Testament the Divine Nature of Jesus, there is again an interruption on the part of the other member of the debate. "Do you mean to say that the *Wisdom of God* is another God?" It is very curious to remark

OF SAPIENTIAL TITLES TO CHRIST

that the equation between Christ and Wisdom is accepted by Zacchaeus. The whole passage is interesting, on account of its parallelism with certain clauses in the Nicene Creed.

Ζακχαῖος εἶπε θέλεις εἰπεῖν ὅτι ἄλλος θεός ἐστιν ἡ σοφία τοῦ Θεοῦ, Ἀθανάσιος εἶπε ἄλλος θεὸς ἐκτὸς τοῦ Θεοῦ οὐκ ἔστιν ὥσπερ οὐδὲ ἄλλο φῶς τὸ ἀπαύγασμα τοῦ φωτός (Sap vii 25) ἀλλὰ φῶς μὲν τὸ φῶς καὶ τὸ ἀπαύγασμα φῶς ἀλλ' οὐχὶ ἄλλο καὶ ἄλλο φῶς οὕτως καὶ ἡ Σοφία τοῦ Θεοῦ

The question as to the nature of the Divine Sophia is raised by Zacchaeus, and answered in terms of the Wisdom of Solomon; that is very significant; for though the final conclusion is that Christ is φῶς ἐκ φωτός as in the Nicene formula, He is also again seen to be Sophia, for He is the ἀπαύγασμα which Wisdom is declared to be.

If we could find out how much of this dialogue is derived from the previous "Jason and Papiscus" we should be able to tell whether the foregoing identifications and their Nicene consequences were trans-Jordanic in their ultimate origin, for the first of the Dialogues in question comes from Pella.

DID JESUS CALL HIMSELF SOPHIA?

As soon as we have decided that behind the Logos-doctrine there lies a more Jewish and less metaphysical Sophia-doctrine, and that the early Christian preaching about Jesus proclaimed Him as the Wisdom of God, we cannot avoid the enquiry whether Jesus identified Himself with the Wisdom of God and announced Himself as such.

The first impulse of response to such an enquiry is to negative the suggestion on the ground (a) that it is inherently improbable, (b) that there is no evidence in support of such an idea either on the Biblical or on the Patristic side. Both of these objections, however, are too à priori. We do not really know without careful enquiry what is likely to have occurred, nor can we tell superficially what is implied in the Biblical and Patristic evidence. We might equally have affirmed that there was no Biblical or Patristic evidence for the substitution of Logos in the place of Sophia, and that it was inherently unlikely that Jesus had been the subject of such a change of title.

Whatever be our views with regard to the nature of the personality of the Lord Jesus, we cannot altogether de-orientalize Him; nor, it might be added, ought we to hyper-philosophize Him. In quite recent times we have had the phenomenon before us of the rise of a new Oriental religion and in the Bâb-movement have been able to detect remarkable analogies to the early Christian history. Probably nothing surprised us more, at the first presentation of the cult to our notice, than the amazing titles given to the leaders of the movement, who would have thought that the end of the nineteenth century could have produced a teacher whose name is *Subh-i-ezel* or *Dawn-of-Eternity*? And as to the adoption of this title by the person himself to whom it was attached, the following note by Professor Browne in his *Episode of the Bâb* (p. 95) may be of interest:

"The name alluded to is of course that of *Ezel* (the Eternal) bestowed on Mirza Yahya by the Bâb. Gobineau calls him *Hazrat-i-Ezel* (L'Altesse Eternelle), but his correct designation, that which he himself adopts, and that whereby he is everywhere known, is *Subh-i-Ezel* (the Morning of Eternity)."

Reasoning from analogy, we may fairly argue that *à priori* objections ought not to settle the question whether Jesus was or was not the *Wisdom of God*: if He was such, there is nothing to prohibit Him from announcing Himself as such, and if, on the other hand, He was merely a teacher who provoked admiring appellations from His followers, as in the case of the leaders of the Bâb movement, or who suggested such appellations to His admiring followers, still there is no *à priori* objection to such a phenomenon amongst the early Christian teachers and leaders. We can, therefore, approach the question whether Jesus called Himself the *Wisdom of God* without the hindrance of antecedent improbability.

One thing seems quite clear: *Jesus did not announce Himself as the Word of God*. That title came from His followers and not from the first generation of them: but since we have shown reason to believe that *Word of God* is a substitute for *Wisdom of God*, it is not unlikely that this latter title, admitted to be antecedent to the second generation of discipleship, may go back to Jesus Himself, for it certainly belongs to the first generation of His followers; and therefore either they gave it to Him or He gave it to Himself. The two things are, in any case, not very far apart chronologically.

DID JESUS CALL HIMSELF SOPHIA?

Another way in which we approach the subject, without wandering off into comparative religion, is to notice how readily we ourselves recover the title when we are speaking in an elevated strain of His Being and Perfections · for example, amongst modern religious writers, one of the illuminated of the last generation was certainly T. T Lynch, both as Preacher and Poet, he says somewhere of Jesus:

> He is the new and ancient Word,
> All Wisdom man hath ever heard
> Hath been both His and He:
> He is the very life of truth,
> In Him it hath eternal youth
> And constant victory

Here the writer has taken his flight from St Augustine's "Beauty, Ancient and yet new," to the Logos, who is also the Eternal Wisdom and the Eternal Truth[1]. And Augustine might be quoted in the very same strain; for he also accepted Wisdom as an Eternal Divine Hypostasis. We may recall that great passage from the conversation at Ostia ·

> We came to our own minds and passed beyond them, that we might arrive at that region of never-failing plenty, where thou feedest Israel for ever with the food of truth, and where Life is the Wisdom by whom all these things were made, both what have been and what shall be, and she herself is not made, but is as she hath been, and so shall be for ever; yea, rather, to have been and hereafter to be are not in her, but only to be, seeing she is eternal.

Evidently St Augustine would have found no difficulty in a statement that "Wisdom was with God and that Wisdom was God". and it was as easy for him as it is possible for us, to recover the lost title "Wisdom of God" for Jesus.

Such a title is almost involved in "the Truth and the Life," which Jesus in the Fourth Gospel affirms Himself to be: but we naturally desire more direct evidence and if possible Synoptic evidence as to the use of the term by Jesus of Himself The passages which Tatian harmonised from Matthew and Luke into

---

[1] It is noteworthy that the same identification occurs in a letter of George Fox to the daughter of Oliver Cromwell

"Then thou wilt feel the power of God, which will bring nature into its course, and give thee to see the glory of the first body There the Wisdom of God will be received, which is Christ, by which all things were made and created, and thou wilt thereby be preserved and ordered to God's glory."

So also C Wesley in a hymn which is headed Prov iii 13, 18:
"Wisdom and Christ and Heaven are one"

the form "therefore, behold! I, the Wisdom of God, send unto you prophets and wise men and scribes," would be decisive if we could be sure that Tatian had recovered the original meaning or given the original sense to the passage of Q which Matthew and Luke are quoting It is not an easy point to settle. It is, however, much more likely that Jesus spoke in the person of the Divine Wisdom, than that the passage is a reference to Scripture either extant or non-extant; and I therefore incline to believe that Tatian has given the sense of the passage. It may be asked why we do not quote the passage in which Jesus declares Himself to be greater, in respect to Wisdom, than Solomon. The answer is that whatever indication may be taken out of these words from Q is negatived by the accompanying statement that Jesus is greater than Jonah If the queen of the south who came to hear the Wisdom of Solomon (Matt. xii 42, Luke xi 31) had stood in a text by herself, without the addition of Jonah and the Ninevites, we might have argued that the Wisdom of Jesus, which He affirmed to be superior to that of Solomon, was the Wisdom of God, and so have looked towards the missing formula that we are in search of It is not safe to lean upon such uncertain evidence

That this Wisdom of Jesus was one of the things that most impressed His contemporaries is evident from the Synoptic tradition,

> Whence hath this man this Wisdom? (Matt. xiii 54, Mark vi 2).

According to Luke he was from his earliest years filled with Wisdom and advancing in the same: but this does not necessarily involve the doctrine that Sophia has descended to dwell amongst us (Luke ii. 40, 52).

St Paul, it should be observed, not only identifies Jesus with the Wisdom and Power of God, but also affirms Him to be the repository of "*all the treasures of Wisdom and Knowledge*" (Col. ii. 3)

The tradition of his Wisdom is conserved for us in a curious Syriac fragment referred to Mara, the son of Serapion, where we are asked "what advantage the Jews derived from the death of *their wise king*, seeing from that time their kingdom was taken away?" (Cureton, *Spicilegium*, p. 72)

No doubt it was by His Wisdom that Jesus impressed His own and succeeding generations

This, however, is insufficient evidence for our purpose Another direction suggests itself, by which we can infer that Jesus identified Himself with the Sophia of the Old Testament It has been from time to time affirmed that the explanation of many of His sayings is to be found in parallel utterances in the Sapiential books; as for instance, that the verses in Matt xi 28–30 are to be traced back to Sirach xxiv. 19, where Sophia says,

> Come unto me all ye that desire me,
> Fill yourselves with my fruits;
> For my memorial is sweeter than honey,
> My inheritance than the honey-comb,

with Sirach h. 26,

> Put your neck under her yoke etc

Similarly it is suggested that the Words of Jesus that

> He that cometh to me shall never hunger,
> He that believeth on me shall never thirst (John vi 35)

are an antithesis to the language of Sophia in Sirach xxiv. 21,

> They that eat me shall hunger again,
> They that drink shall thirst again.

If we could be sure that we had traced these sayings of Jesus to their proximate original, it would be easy to infer that He had borrowed the language of Sophia and was speaking in her person This would very nearly settle the question that we are investigating. Jesus would be Sophia because His invitations would be those of Sophia

In this direction it is possible that further illumination may be forthcoming

Meanwhile we have got far enough in the enquiry to see how completely off the mark was Dr Plummer in his commentary on Luke in the passages under discussion. He tells us:

Nowhere does he style himself "The Wisdom of God," nor does any evangelist give him this title, nor does θεοῦ σοφίαν or σοφία ἀπὸ θεοῦ (1 Cor. i. 24, 30) warrant us in asserting that this was a common designation among the first Christians so that tradition might have substituted this name for ἐγώ used by Jesus... Rather it is of the Divine Providence (Prov. viii. 22–31) sending Prophets to the Jewish Church and Apostles to the Christian Church, that Jesus here speaks, "God in his wisdom said."

In view of the preceding investigations which we have made into the origin of the Logos-Doctrine, it appears that we might contradict almost every one of the statements here made· or at least we might say, in imitation of the language of Ignatius, πρόκειται, "that is the very point at issue": and if it is conceded that it was Wisdom of the eighth chapter of Proverbs that is responsible for sending prophets and Apostles, we have given abundant reason for believing that Jesus was, by the first generation of His followers, identified with this very Wisdom. In that case, ἐγώ and Σοφία are interchangeable, at least in the mind of His adherents, and perhaps in His own.

ST JOHN AND THE DIVINE WISDOM

It has been shown in many ways that the identification of Christ with the Wisdom of God is fundamental in the primitive collection of *Testimonies* employed in the propaganda of the first Christian teachers. It was the first article of the Christian theology, so far as that theology is involved in the archetype of the collection of *Testimonies* made by Cyprian, and it can be shown to be equally involved in a variety of Christian writings In a previous chapter we have pointed out that the Cyprianic chapter that "Christ is the hand and arm of God" has behind it the doctrine that "Sophia is the hand of God." There can be no doubt that in the primitive *Testimony Book* Christ was equated with *Sophia*

If, then, we can show that the Fourth Gospel betrays a direct dependence upon the Apostolic collection of *Testimonies*, we shall then be entitled to affirm that the writer was acquainted with the Sophia-Christ equation and that he made his Logos-Christ equation in view of the previous identification, which he must consequently have modified. This is what we have to prove. It is *à priori* probable that the case was as we suggest, for if the *Testimony Book* antedates the Pauline Epistles, it antedates the Fourth Gospel; and as it was certainly an apostolic document, it would not be surprising for the author of the Fourth Gospel to be acquainted with it.

An actual proof that this was the case may be obtained by studying the sequence and argument of John xii 37-40. The writer has been recording the increasing alienation between Jesus and the Jews, until he comes to the point where Jesus is obliged to go into hiding to escape the hostility of the unbelieving Jews.

ST JOHN AND THE DIVINE WISDOM 63

At this point he stops his narration in order to point out, that it had been predicted that they would not believe in Him, for had it not been written by Isaiah as follows:

> Who hath believed our report,
> And to whom hath the arm of the Lord been revealed? (Is. liii. 1).

And the Jewish unbelief was inevitable, for had not Isaiah also said,

> He hath blinded their eyes (Is vi 9, 10)?

So the question arises naturally, whether these anti-Judaic verses belong to a primitive collection of *Testimonia adversus Judaeos*.

In order to answer this question we turn in the first instance to Cyprian.

He quotes Is. liii. 1 twice over in the *Testimonia*, once to prove that *Christ is the arm of the Lord* ("to whom is the arm of the Lord revealed?"), and once to prove that *Christ is lowly in His first advent*, where Cyprian goes on to prove that Jesus is the root out of a dry ground, etc In neither of these passages, however, is there an immediate reference to the unbelief of the Jews. We should have expected the quotation to occur in the first book of the *Testimonia* under some such heading as that

> it had been foretold that they would not know the Lord nor understand.

And we think it must actually have stood there, for in that very section stands the second Johannine reference, as follows:

> Vade et dic populo isto: aure audietis et non intellegetis et uidentes uidebitis et non uidebitis incrassauit enim cor populi eius, et auribus grauiter audierunt, et oculos suos concluserunt, ne forte uideant oculis et auribus audiant et corde intellegant et curem illos (Cyp *Test*. i. 3).

Both of the Johannine quotations are, then, in the *Testimony Book* according to Cyprian, and one of them is in its right place. We may, therefore, say that John xii. 38–40 has all the appearance of being taken from a collection of *Testimonies*. Very good! but then we are face to face with the fact that the extract given above from Cyprian does not agree with

> τετύφλωκεν αὐτῶν τοὺς ὀφθαλμούς,
> καὶ ἐπώρωσεν αὐτῶν τὴν καρδίαν,
> ἵνα μὴ ἴδωσιν τοῖς ὀφθαλμοῖς,
> καὶ νοήσωσιν τῇ καρδίᾳ καὶ στραφῶσιν,
> καὶ ἰάσομαι αὐτούς

while it does agree almost exactly with the LXX and with the Greek of Matt xiii. 14, 15 and of the Acts xxviii. 26, 27, in both of which cases in the N.T. the passage is employed in an anti-Judaic sense.

Nor is this variation of John from the LXX the only thing to be noted in the history of this famous quotation. It occurs in Justin Martyr, to whom we must now turn In two strongly anti-Judaic passages in his *Dialogue with Trypho* Justin tells his Jewish audience as follows:

(a) *Dial.* c 12   τὰ ὦτα ὑμῶν πέφρακται,
οἱ ὀφθαλμοὶ ὑμῶν πεπήρωνται,
καὶ πεπάχυνται ἡ καρδία
(b) *Dial* c 33   τὰ δὲ ὦτα ὑμῶν πέφρακται,
καὶ αἱ καρδίαι πεπήρωνται.

The two passages are fragments of the same tradition, the second of the two having got into confusion through dropping a clause

We have now three forms of the passage from Isaiah before us, one of which is the plain Septuagint text; the other two may be taken, following Papias' suggestion, as independent modifications of a primitive Aramaic. If this be the correct explanation, we must be right in saying that John knew and used the *Book of Testimonies*; and he could hardly have done this without knowing its leading proposition that Jesus is the Wisdom of God[1].

The point reached by our investigation appears to mark an advance in the following sense. Two fresh facts (hitherto unnoticed or almost unobserved) have come to light: first that the tradition of the *Testimony Book* is earlier than the New Testament, antedates the Gospels, is Apostolic in origin, and the common property of all schools of Christian thought   Second, in accordance with the tradition of the *Testimony Book*, as well as from several other lines of enquiry, it is clear that the first and foremost article of Christian belief is that *Jesus is the Wisdom of God*, personified, incarnate, and equated with every form of personification of

---

[1] There is still something queer about the two Justinian forms (a) and (b). If we read πεπώρωνται in (b) we are much nearer to the Johannine form. But then what becomes of form (a)? Shall we read

τὰ ὦτα ὑμῶν πέφρακται,
οἱ ὀφθαλμοὶ ὑμῶν πεπήρωνται,
καὶ πεπώρωται ἡ καρδία,

and treat πεπάχυνται as introduced from the LXX?

The variations in the text of Isaiah as quoted are a sufficient evidence of the wide diffusion of the *Testimony*

On the other hand, the evidence of the Oxyrhynchus *Fragments of Sayings of Jesus* ("They are blind in their heart") is in favour of attaching πεπώρωται to καρδία.

ST JOHN AND THE DIVINE WISDOM

Wisdom that could be derived from or suggested by the Scriptures of the Old Testament. Upon the recognition and right evaluation of these two facts our reconstruction of the theology of the first age of the Church will depend. Here is a simple instance, to conclude with, to show the re-action of the argument upon the interpretation of the Epistles

The recognition of the Sapiential origin of the appellation of Christ in the first chapter of Colossians will help us to the understanding of a passage in Romans, where we are told that believers are fore-ordained to a conformity to the image ($\varepsilon i\kappa\acute{\omega}\nu$) of the Son of God, so that He may be the first-born ($\pi\rho\omega\tau\acute{o}\tau o\kappa o\varsigma$) among many brethren Here the apparatus of the reader of the New Testament naturally suggests for the 'first-born' a reference to Colossians: but since in Colossians 1 15, 16, we have the sequence

Image ($\varepsilon i\kappa\acute{\omega}\nu$) of the invisible God;
First-born ($\pi\rho\omega\tau\acute{o}\tau o\kappa o\varsigma$) of all creation;

it is natural to suggest that in Romans 1. 29 we have a similar transition. That is to say, we must put a comma after $\varepsilon i\kappa\acute{o}\nu o\varsigma$ and read $\tau o\hat{\upsilon}$ $\upsilon i o\hat{\upsilon}$ $a\dot{\upsilon}\tau o\hat{\upsilon}$ in apposition to it:

that we may be conformed to *the Image*,
i e to His Son,
that the Son may be *the First-born*,
i e. among many brethren

NOTE.

ORIGEN AND THE SAPIENTIAL CHRIST.

The doctrine that Christ is the ἀπόρροια of God appears again in Origen in the following form.
Comm. in ep. ad Romanos.
vii. 13. Unus autem uterque est Deus, quia non est aliud Filio divinitatis initium quam Pater; sed ipsius unius Paterni fontis (sicut Sapientia dicit) purissima est manatio Filius. Est ergo Christus *Deus super omnia* Quae omnia? Illa sine dubio quae et paulo ante diximus, Eph. i. 21. Qui autem super omnia est, super se neminem habet Non enim post Patrem est ipse, sed de Patre Hoc idem autem Sapientia Dei etiam de Spiritu Sancto intelligi dedit, ubi dicit· Spiritus Domini, etc. (Sap. i. 7)

Here it is clear that Origen is finding Christ in the Wisdom of Solomon, and that one of his identifications is that Christ is the ἀπόρροια or *manatio* This identification is important for its theological value and for its literary interest. The Fathers commonly take it to mean an outflow of light from a source of light, which leads us to the Nicene formula; but in the literature of the early Church it appears as an irresistible flow of water, as in the sixth Ode of Solomon; where, by the way, the Gnostic author of the *Pistis Sophia* changes the explanation to an emanation of light.

www.ingramcontent.com/pod-product-compliance
Lightning Source LLC
Chambersburg PA
CBHW071746040426
42446CB00012B/2478